PEARLS ON A STRING

FURTHER EXTENDING HEALTH (AND RETIREMENT) SAVINGS ACCOUNTS

George Ross Fisher, M.D.

Printed in the United States of America

Library of Congress Copyright: 1-2540412791

ISBN: 978-1-932080-56-8
Ross & Perry Book Publishers
3 South Haddon Avenue
Haddonfield, New Jersey 08033
856-427-6135

Also by the same author:

The Hospital That Ate Chicago, Saunders Press, 1980
Health Savings Accounts: Planning for Prosperity, Ross & Perry, Inc. 2015
*Surmounting Health Costs to Retire: Health
(and Retirement) Savings Account,* 2016

Acknowledgements

For advice and support about the thrust of this much revised book, I owe new debts to the many people who read the first versions and commented. The first book was written as ideas developed in my mind, and rather in a hurry. The second revision was written so later thoughts could be introduced earlier in the argument. This one was written and rewritten to rise above the twin possibilities that either, the Affordable Care Act would be completely repealed, or it would essentially survive forever. I still don't know its future, whether it is too big to fail, or too big to survive. Either way, I think it failed to reform some things which should be reformed. The best way to defend that position is to propose an alternative which is much simpler, but more radical.

Dedication

To Senator Bill Roth of Delaware, who demonstrated the road between private and public sectors, need not be a one-way street.

Table of Contents

Introduction

Pearls on a String: Further Extending Health (and Retirement) Savings Accounts. HSAs are the string. Retirement saving, Privatizing Medicare, and Shifting Childhood Costs-- are the Pearls. Other Pearls to follow.

The waste in the medical system is mainly a result of poor coordination of its finance design with its central -- medical -- functions. This in turn is partly a result of adopting specialized independent functions, and greatly exaggerated by imposing the third-party (insurance) system between them. And partly it grows out of a mistaken business-school doctrine that all businesses are the same, regardless of their product. The consequence has been the interposition of two business-school organizations between the patient and his doctor. An unexpected but visible consequence has been a spectacular widening between costs and prices. It symbolizes the collision between the business plan to make a profit, and the Hippocratic Oath to place patient benefit ahead of personal gain. Like a spoiled child, the public demands unreasonable success with unreasonably low prices. The bizarre result has been an unsustainable set of internal cross subsidies, held together by the illusion that moral justification is a permanent justification for economic absurdity.

This book has attempted to devise a goal and a way to reach it with stretched-out pre-payment in the hands of the patient. But the longer a change is drawn out, the more chance of misjudgment and what you seek most to avoid -- the pain of sudden collapse. The implicit cost has grown so large it could require a century to absorb it. And so the central question emerges as to how much shorter for safety the transition really needs to be. If we crash along the way, it is proof we waited too long. So what we might attempt needs to be better understood. We have developed a system of intimidating our leaders, to the point they are afraid to do the right thing. So the public demands even more vigorous creative destruction. This is your last chance, is what they seem willing to threaten.

My answer is it is impossible to answer in advance how long the transition should be, before we take the final leap. It is only possible to estimate, by experience, how much steady progress toward the goal is possible. It is only possible to know what rate of progress toward the goal, for what sustainable spurts of time, is enough to satisfy the public, that their leaders even approximately know where they are going.

Prologue:
Broadened Vistas for Health Financing

Overview. To be brief about it, spending for healthcare now crowds toward the end of life, mostly after age 65, while the money to pay for it is generated well before 65. Disregarding the complicated history of how we got here, in effect we borrow from an interest-free account at Medicare to pay Medicare for Medicare, without earning interest on the money idled in the meantime, sometimes for as long as forty years. Potentially, the two age groups could unify their finances and get more or less dual savings. That's the dream advanced by the single payer advocates, but on examination the cost, politics, and complexities of actually unifying entire delivery systems would soon overwhelm total- merger enthusiasts. Unfortunately, the revenue has fallen too far behind the costs to make this completely possible. It is nevertheless contended here, only the financial transfers need to be unified, using Health Savings Accounts as a transfer vehicle, and allowing compound interest to extend beyond the boundaries of insurance programs. Such simplification, while not easy, would achieve most of the savings of unifying whole insurance programs, particularly the incentive to keep what you don't use, for your retirement. Among other things, it would solve most of the Constitutional problems, and avoids most of the delivery system obstacles. Indeed, a financial network is about all we could manage, but it is adequate for the need. Because of its towering cost components, even integrating the financial transfers might take longer than we anticipate.

But massive numbers are only part of the health financing problem. At the beginning of life, medical expenses concentrate forward, toward the very first day, leaving absolutely no way for the child's own income to pre-pay his expenses. No matter how it is rearranged,

1

someone must give children some money. Indeed, this second issue seems so unsolvable, everyone has stopped trying to notice it. It only makes people uncomfortable to suggest that adding children to a new HSA system might add twenty-some years to the compound interest in Health Savings Accounts, if they only had some money. They don't, so be quiet.

But on the contrary, if someone always gives children the money for their healthcare, why not acknowledge it? Frank acknowledgement seems pre-destined, if you aspire to serve lifetime financing. You require two systems, roughly the opposite of each other. One delivery system faces toward the beginning and the other, faces toward the end of life. (Even this conception finds the working class in the middle, largely funded by employers who change frequently and have other concerns foremost in their minds.) If the realities of life will never change, then it is the payment system which must adjust, with the finances of each system facing in opposite ways. The reader is therefore urged to toy with the eventual outline of a circular system, far down the line. For now, existing programs would alter their interface to accommodate a new funds flow, while changing their program as little as possible. There's still a big gap left unfilled: Those working people aged 25-65 who largely support the whole system, unfortunately already have so many constraints on their financing it is not feasible even to discuss their needs until the politics subside a little. Connecting, yes; unifying, only as much as you can. Therefore, this book passes over single payer as fundamentally over-reaching and concentrates on lower-hanging fruit.

Essentially, it is proposed: The Health Savings Account to expand to be a unifying financial bridge between programs, one account per individual lifetime, serving many disparate programs. Designed to be implemented in phased-in pieces, it continues to aspire to minimize changes in the delivery system itself. The reader will probably be surprised at how simple some dilemmas are likely to become, once it is conceded the individual patient ought to decide what others now decide for him.

Prepare yourself for one big rearrangement of thinking, however.

Extended retirement costs are a direct consequence of superior healthcare. They could become five times as expensive as healthcare itself, and still be fairly described as a predictable outcome cost of Medicare. The only way budget shifts could be avoided is if science cures a few expensive diseases, quickly. That's not impossible, but it's unwise to depend on. It's also conceivable Medicare beneficiaries could be persuaded to allow HSAs to borrow from Medicare, but only after a titanic struggle, and only after Medicare revenues improve appreciably. New revenues for retirement must nevertheless be found, sooner rather than later, because of the ever-growing retirement crunch. It's a devastating realization, but the seed of solving the problem is contained in it. Where are the new revenues to come from?

> Extended retirement costs are a predictable outcome cost of Medicare.

SECTION ONE:

HEALTH SAVINGS ACCOUNTS, NOT SO BAD BY THEMSELVES

HSA becomes HRSA, Then Emerges as the String that Threads the Pearls

The book before you is not a list of dooms and glooms, it turns into a proposal. A proposal to preserve a functioning society by regarding child, parent, and grandparent as different stages of the same person's life, with united interest in the same goal. The same goal, even for a newborn, is a comfortable retirement. While it speaks exclusively to paying for healthcare, the same principles apply to any useful but expensive commodity. That is, as much as possible, individuals subsidizing themselves at different ages rather than members of three different classes of strangers. We build upon the idea of a Health Savings Account, one account per person throughout one lifetime, as a financial way to emphasize the underlying social point. If you spend too much too early, you won't have much left for later. That sounds far less obvious when it appears within separate compartments, with separate sources of funding. Separate sources have their own budgets coming first in their minds. They compete with each other for the same money, if they can.

This unification proposal -- Pearls on a String -- is voluntary, you don't have to do it, or even part of it, but in some ways that's another advantage. True, there is no escaping the use of insurance for unexpected catastrophes, but really, only an insurance salesman would argue for unlimited insurance for everyone, all the time. Only someone who knows very little about insurance would believe insurance is a way of printing money for the customer. Compulsory also means uniform, government-issue. Voluntary, by contrast, isn't a one-size-fits-all commitment, and doesn't dump 340 million subscribers onto inadequately tested systems, all at once.

Whether voluntary or mandatory however, some facts are just part of life. Almost completely, the working generation must subsidize its older and younger generations, but it would do it better with a focus on the same individual at different ages, instead of by whole categories of strangers. For a final twist, we unexpectedly propose to empower solutions by leveraging a new problem we scarcely noticed we had (prolonged longevity and retirement). It isn't a trick; in retrospect, everything looks as though it might have been predicted.

Three New Potentials. Curiously, the Health Savings Account had to be tested before it could be fully understood even by its originators. A bit of history may help explain the delay. The basic concept of Health Savings Accounts was developed in 1981 by John McClaughry and me, while John was Senior Policy Advisor in the Reagan White House. Derived from the IRA concept developed by Senator Bill Roth of Delaware, it started like a Christmas Savings Account, to save up for the approaching deductible of (high-deductible) Catastrophic health insurance -- which was to be linked to it. So from its beginning there were two linked features: (1) a high-deductible health insurance, and (2) a medical variant of an Individual Retirement Account (IRA). For those unfamiliar with insurance jargon, a high "front-end" deductible policy connotes the insurance company only insures that part of a medical bill which is *greater than the stated deductible amount*.

Since this automatically means the higher the deductible, the lower the annual insurance premium; high deductible policies are the cheapest you can buy. When the Affordable Care Act was passed, all health insurance was required to have a "high" deductible, so the HSA idea then seemed moot. But a high deductible by itself isn't enough. Without the savings account attached to it the client can't easily separate risk protection from pre-payment, or for that matter inpatient costs from outpatient ones. Ideally, the level of the chosen deductible is the result of tension between a high level to please the insurance company, and a low level to attract the customer. Call it luck or call it planning, a high deductible separates inpatient from outpatient, market prices versus fixed ones, optional costs from unavoidable ones, prevention from treatment, and risk protection from pre-payment. Out of these segregations, remarkable things can be achieved. The one danger is that the deductible might fail to change with circumstances. The divisions are set by the market balance between customer and provider, and are rough ones. If either side succeeds in freezing the deductible, its underlying significance could disappear.

After experience in action, a totally new realization dawned that -- once the two parts became semi-independent -- the real deductible just becomes the unpaid portion of it. The unpaid portion of the deductible is now situated in the account, ultimately becoming zero -- but now *the insurance premium no longer rises as the remaining deductible declines.* Not at first but eventually, the HSA emerges looking like "first-dollar coverage" for the same low price as high-deductible insurance. The truth is, you have two insurance policies, one owned by the insurance company, and the deductible, which is self-insured, owned by yourself.

The higher the deductible, the lower the yearly insurance premium.

You can be as frivolous or as frugal as you please, within the self-insured deductible. The insurance could care less which it is. A great many people have no medical expenses for a whole year, so they get to keep all of it. Someone else could spend it all. Another way of saying this is, saving for the deductible has shifted into the customer's own hands without shifting any extra burden onto an insurance company. A mandatory expense now transforms into part of his disposable income. Frivolous (ie small) expenses are self-insured; necessary ones (ie expensive ones) are insurance-insured. It wasn't exactly the deductible that saved money, it was the new-found ability to exclude non-essential expenses if you chose to.

A second realization emerges from the tendency of non-insurance HSA managers to use debit cards for medical reimbursement, instead of insurance claims forms. (This freedom may well be a consequence of concentrating frivolous expenses into the deductible.) Although in the absence of strict scrutiny there might well be more temptation to cheat, a debit-card system depends on the client to howl if he suspects his money is being mis-spent. Otherwise, it will be lost. (When you spend a third party's money, there's less concern than in spending your own.) A decline of policing cost might even be said to expose *a lack of overall effectiveness of the third-party approach to policing of claims.* Since it is obviously more costly to police than not to police, that particular hidden cost of using third parties only emerges after it gets eliminated. (This same reasoning applies to a diagnosis-based payment for helpless hospital inpatients, a related issue which is now segregated into the insurance compartment of HSAs, but crippled by the crudeness of its DRG coding system.)

The foregoing describes two potentials, broader coverage and less administrative cost, but an even more gratifying development might be a decline in elective claims, despite reduced cost-containment effort. This is harder to prove, but highly likely. At first, this likely saving seemed attributable to the ("adverse") selection of unusually frugal applicants. But over time, a more likely incentive emerged: added provisions of the HSA act permitted any surplus remaining at age 65 to be turned into an Individual Retirement Account. That is, *an incentive was created to save health money for retirement, by substituting personal responsibility for insurance company vigilance.* All in all, it would not be a bad outcome. So far as I know, it is the only form of health insurance which has this feature, which every one of them ought to use, by means of attaching their "bead" to the "string". All other health insurance returns a surplus to lowering the costs for others; that only works if you never change companies, and even then, the temptation of management to skim it is undeniable.

A second implication of this third zinger in the system took even longer to sink in, because nobody wanted to believe it. It suggested our path might never lead us out of the financial hole we were in. Not eventually, but never. The situation was this: As improved health care spread among the elderly, the elderly lived longer. Gradually and grudgingly, it was acknowledged *extended longevity was a hidden cost of Medicare, unanticipated perhaps, but universal.* Its pain first started to hurt beyond the insurance boundary, accounting for delay in recognition of the link. There was Social Security of course, left in the dust of thirty years of longevity added since 1900. Increased longevity was first discovered as destroying the attractiveness of defined-benefit retirements. But as it became acknowledged that good health and longer longevity were two

HSAs are the only health insurance with the incentive to save for retirement whatever you don't spend for healthcare.

manifestations of the same effort, the doubled cost began to be seen as insupportable. What's worse, the future cost of retirement is even harder to specify than the future cost of health care, because everyone has his own definition of a "decent" retirement. Underfunded retirement is an even stronger incentive to watch your pennies than a specified one, because there is absolutely no one, not even that demonized one percent of rich folks, who can be certain there will be enough money left at the end, to last out his lifetime. Wasn't that combined incentive enough to get everybody's attention?

The Driving Force. For the purposes of this book, the power of that unfunded retirement incentive was the HSA's most important new insight. Almost anybody could tell at a glance the high cost of Medicare was what stopped "single payer" in its tracks, what paralyzed Congress on healthcare, and defied solutions from any other direction. Medicare was the "third rail" of politics -- touch it and you're dead. But with a retirement entitlement looming behind it almost making Medicare costs seem laughable, it was a new ball game. Once retirement begins, retirement savings get steadily depleted, whereas serious health costs are usually episodic. Both begin at the same time.

Six conclusions emerge:

1. The Health Savings Account, as is, is quite adequate (if funded, or course) to cover healthcare costs in replacement of existing health insurance. It's surely cheaper, although possibly not as much as the 30% reported in early trials. There are several reasons why that should always remain the case, although it does require more management by the customer. It is entirely suitable for intermittent use as employers and government programs change.

2. The HSA already contains the mechanism of the customer funding up to its present $3400 yearly limit, with annual cost of living adjustments but excluding the cost of the attached health insurance, gathering investment income for decades, and turning it over at age 65 as an IRA retirement fund. In honor of this feature, it is proposed to rename HSA to HRSA (Health, and Retirement, Savings Account.) As such, it would supplement any other retirement source, but could

stand alone. Its main flaw is easily corrected; the law limits coverage to employed people. No children, no supplements after age 65, but that would be simple to fix. There is a political risk in allowing the annual deposit limits to be at the mercy of changing political administrations.

3. New means of investment, such as passive investment of total market index funds, seem as safe as most investments now offered. Cheaper ways to increase effective returns should be explored, particularly in dividing returns between HSA management and their customers. I suggest published "fee only" arrangements would give the public a chance to shop around. Later on, ways might be explored to balance voting power in health companies against the medical prices reflected in the price of their stock. Demonstration projects might be in order. Present owners of HSAs will probably be shocked to hear the total market has averaged 11% returns during the Obama eight years; how many HSAs paid customers more than 3%?

4. With minor legal adjustments, the HSA could serve as the investment conduit for: surplus generated by Medicare, a proposed Childhood Transfer System, an end of life reinsurance system (to be described), and any other health program which changes its proposals to transfer surpluses to retirement, as an incentive to become a frugal shopper. For the time being, however, it is intended to remain entirely independent of the Affordable Care Act until politics clarify.

5. The ultimate goal is to construct a lifetime framework for HSAa, to serve as a financial vehicle for connecting all health plans around a common investment and retirement framework. It might easily include such things as bounties for below-average health expenditures and rewards for superior performance of other sorts.

6. The longer-term goal is to re-arrange pieces of this network to increase investment returns, starting with Medicare (see below), Last Four Years of Life Reinsurance and First Twenty-five Years Gift Transfers, with the rest of life added, accordion-style. These terms should become clearer after later discussion.

In the existing environment, third party reimbursement of healthcare now stands in the road of everybody's retirement, by being disjointed. That's not to suggest unifying whole programs, an overwhelming task, but merely to unify their transfers and their retirement termination, as well as the age and employment limitations of individual pieces. So long as left-overs ultimately belong to the individual, and the separate pieces are all available for compound interest along the way, the affiliations can be quite loose. On the other hand, if further program integration seems cost-effective, nothing stands in its way.

Medicare's financing problems might even became a symbol the problem was not just a lobbying benefit to be defended blindly by its current beneficiaries. Increased retirement cost was, in short, an overlooked cost of health care all along, and anyone who stood in the way of coordinating things has misjudged the ultimate necessities. Standing closest to retirement, Medicare is in fact the very first program you must change. But you better do it very carefully. And by the way, you better do it pretty soon.

The Grand Plan for HRSA Networks, Very Briefly

So, we discover Health Savings Accounts are not snake-oil, a quick-fix solution to every healthcare problem ever complained about. No good idea is improved by such exaggeration. What is offered here is a long-term plan for greatly reducing the cost of healthcare, conceivably cutting it in half. It has some features which would show quick results, and we must devise a transition plan which puts them first. But it might take fifty years to achieve it all, and much can happen to upset plans in fifty years. The plan of this book is to suggest what should be done, in more or less the order of when to do it. But first to sketch in -- very briefly -- the final goals for doing any of it.

What Have Your Done for Me, Lately? What I propose is a healthcare network of existing systems, linked together one by one with the retirement and investment incentives of Health (and Retirement) Savings Accounts. The short term value of the network is to create a unified transfer system to the more distant goals, providing some time to reach them. The HSA will be tempted to wander from its mission, but should remain as simple as possible -- a gussied-up transfer vehicle for healthcare funds. Most of the elements are in place for this, although some enabling amendments might be suggested. Meanwhile, the option must persist for using HRSAs by themselves as total lifetime coverage, since transitional changes may leave some people without suitable alternatives. But repairing existing programs rather than replacing them--Medicare, in particular--usually offers the advantage of shortening the transition time. The long transition period is certainly what people will find hardest to accept.

With the framework in place, the institutions attached to it should be gradually coaxed into externalizing their surpluses (dividends or their equivalent) instead of re-investing them, allowing surplus to flow between low-cost and high-cost eras of consumers' lives within the network, ultimately ending up as individual retirement financing in the private sector. That last part may be hard for people working in the public sector to accept, because it removes the government as insurer of last resort for pensions. But for reasons too obscure to describe here, that was never possible as long as Congress controlled the extension of national debt. And that in turn was driven by the conviction the private sector was a superior creator of wealth, not an unlimited source of taxes. Ultimately, our model is the goose that laid golden eggs.

An easy early step would be to create following-year bonuses for low expenditures within the "pearls" on this string. Much will depend on intervening national politics, and it is intended to avoid including ACA or employer-based insurance until the direction clarifies. Meanwhile, everyone might have the option of adopting an HRSA fully, plus Medicare, plus the childhood transfer mechanism. The ultimate unified vehicle would be an accordion-structured First and Last Years of Life Reinsurance (see below), although if several variants emerge, that would be fine.

The final step, **integrating the ACA and present employer-based systems** is left entirely out of the project for the first few years. But driving it onward, posing the threat of retirement destitution if you don't, would be the availability of retirement financing from every penny you legitimately save from healthcare, from the day of birth to the day of death. Since no one wants to die, and very few enjoy living in poverty, restraining this vast incentive must rest with its health beneficiaries, since everyone is its ultimate beneficiary. When scientists finally do cure the worst diseases cheaply, the retirement folks may be permitted to start to win the healthcare vs. retirement pension competition.

Special projects and program outliers, such as prison inmates, mentally and physically disabled, and illegal immigrants, are left for us to find solutions more tailored to their needs, and here are not dealt with further. This proposal deals with the great majority of Americans who are not in poverty, not handicapped, and not poorly treated. Surely they should have a voice in such a vital topic, which from their perspective could be considerably cheaper, and rather easily improved over present uncertainties. Along the way, if they themselves could devise something beyond golf, bridge, gardening and travel to occupy thirty years, it would be an enhancement to the community. Arguments can be made for regulating immigration, but not ones for providing servants for a rentier society.

We begin integration with the big gorilla, Medicare. In the first place, the program is bleeding money. The first step in saving money should be to stop losing so much of it, and that definitely won't be easy as long as serious illness keeps migrating into the Medicare age group. Furthermore, it contains the most expensive item of all, terminal care. The transfer of terminal care out of Medicare by the Last Four Years of Life transfer, should facilitate this decision. Other programs may get financially healthier if we do nothing. If we do nothing about Medicare, it probably will only get into deeper trouble.

At the moment, our best dream is the scientists will find something as cheap as an aspirin, which will cure something as expensive as cancer. A century ago and roughly simultaneously, scientists discovered cures for pernicious anemia and type I diabetes, both fatal conditions. Pernicious anemia has virtually disappeared with occasional injections of a vitamin, while diabetes has grown to be about as expensive as anything, despite lifesaving injections of insulin. Unless you want to gamble on similar mixed outcomes in the future, read on.

SECTION TWO

THREE MORE PEARLS, MAKES FOUR

The Segments of Lifetime Healthcare: Medicare Including Retirement Pearl #1

The Affordable Care Act was announced as mandating health insurance for everyone, but about thirty million people were specifically excluded. The healthcare problems of seven million prison inmates, eight million unemployables, and eleven million illegal immigrants were too specialized to be included in a program which hoped to be one-size fits all. Quite properly, such **special outliers** would be better handled by special programs designed for their special needs.

The Affordable Care Act (ACA) is now central to Administration attention, and Medicare may be deemed too hot to handle in an election campaign. Nevertheless, we elected here to discuss Medicare but not the ACA. Retirement, childhood, and how to unify complete the list--pretty much all that's left surrounding, but excluding the ACA, election or no election. That emphasizes what had been evaded or neglected, and avoids direct confrontation with the ACA, preparing for the day when that big gorilla is either confirmed or abandoned. It's obviously too expensive, and it remains to be seen whether it can be fixed, or must be abandoned. **In our alternative scheme,** all of lifetime healthcare would be financially connected to a single lifetime Health Savings Account, one account per person, but the delivery systems would remain semi-autonomous. ACA could surely live in peace with the HRSAs, and could even peacefully adopt the HSA approach. That would save money, but the questions left are whether it would save enough to be worth the trouble, and whether politics will allow it. Like the European Union, it's surely easier to describe than to accomplish.

Retirement as a Medical Issue. The news is precarious for retirement funding. We begin with the far end of life, where most health cost and all retirement cost concentrates. While retirement is parallel in time to Medicare, we begin to recognize increased longevity as an outcome

21

of better health. If one is to help pay for the other, they must, in the Medicare case, draw their funds from the same pool. That's Medicare, which most people don't want to change, but is the first thing which must change. Because unchanged it costs too much to leave anything for retirement.

Although the Industrial Revolution brought many lifestyle improvements in the past two centuries, it also brought turmoil. The idea of leisure time may once have been a reward for the upper 1%, but actually most of the population never dreamed of any leisure time. The novels of the "Lost Generation" after the first World War often revolved around the discovery of unfamiliar leisure pursuits by members of social classes newly learning about such things. The moral, then and now, seems to be that leisure is no bed of roses.

We must assign a reasonable definition to a "decent" retirement, provide for a marginal one, and leave the rest to our own sources of wealth.

The cultural response seems to be that leisure was best reserved for retirement, although the younger generation sometimes rebelled, wanting some of it sooner. In any event, Medicare surely extended retirement longevity. (Overextended it, if you believe it will be impossible to pay for.) After all, retirement is a continuous cost, while illness is episodic. There are ways of calculating costs which depict retirement as five times as expensive as healthcare. But Medicare cost averages thirteen thousand dollars a year, and rising. That's a pretty meager retirement, and when you discover Medicare is 50% borrowed, you question how many people could retire on $26,000 a year per person, on public sector revenues. If you see retirement as a couple of old folks, you wonder where they would get $52,000 a year, for thirty years. Add Medicare to retirement, and you begin to get absolutely impossible numbers. There seems no possible way to handle this except to provide for subsistence retirement, plus Medicare, and let everyone find some way to get whatever extra he needs, or defines as "decent". And that defines retirement cost as equal to medical costs, when both costs could rise appreciably. The Health Savings Account method of accomplishing this is to put retirement at the end of the financial line, funded by the residuals of the other pearls on the string. You keep what's left. Another way is to retire later, or best of all, find some remunerative way to fill your time and use your experience.

Medicare As a Financial Issue. Medicare is about half paid-for, half borrowed, but it's really totally under water. According to Mrs. Sibelius, about half of Medicare expenditures are supported by the general fund, or general taxation. The general fund is in deficit, however, providing some fairness to the description of Medicare as a fund borrowed from the Chinese, although China and Japan combined only purchase 13% of ten-year Treasury bonds. In the event of Medicare default, the main creditor victims will be U.S. citizens. The purchasers may change, but the deficit looks to be permanent. Until deficits are paid off, it will remain true that Medicare provides a dollar of care for fifty cents. That sounds wonderful, until it suddenly sounds terrible. Medicare is bleeding money. If you want to know how brutal our government can get, read the section later on, about the Diagnosis Related Groups.

About half of the Medicare deficit is pay as you go, about another half is borrowed; only a quarter of the budget is current revenue from the beneficiary age group.

An accountant might say, **Medicare's cash revenue** is roughly divided between premiums paid by the beneficiaries, and pre-paid as a payroll tax of 3% on workers not yet old enough for benefits. (About half of this wage tax comes directly from the employee, another half from the employer. We skip over the technicalities that some parts of the program are tied to one fund, other parts to another, and also some are subject to higher income tax). About a quarter of Medicare is paid in advance on a "pay-as-you-go" basis, which is to say some people pay current costs of other people -- they are definitely not saved in anticipation of the contributors becoming beneficiaries, as the term "Trust Fund" implies.

A second quarter is indeed paid and spent by current beneficiaries as Medicare premiums. That is, *about half of the deficit is pay as you go, another half is borrowed from foreigners; only half of the deficit is matched by current revenue from the beneficiary age group.* Nevertheless, the payers of pay-as-you-go are about thirty years younger than the spenders of it. If we put the youngsters' cash to work for thirty years, what interest rate would it take to grow one dollar into three?

The answer is about five to seven percent. For quicker understanding, a few unfamiliar tools are needed:

First and Last Years of Life Re-Insurance By far the best proposal for refinancing Medicare, however, is to anticipate the way science is going to re-design costs. In the long, long, run, there should be very little medical cost left, except the first and last years of life. We have no idea how long it will take, but that's the direction things are almost sure to be going.

So, **phase in a re-structuring of funding for both children and elderly first, and then add in the rest of a lifespan, step by step**. That way, you first fund an obligation you are always sure to have. Be sure to do it in such a way that maximizes the investment income at compound interest. This might be a project under construction for decades, but its first step would be to begin funding for the Last Four Years of Life, which happens to be an early proposal in refinancing Medicare. Since the reader may be unprepared for the topic, it is considered in a free-standing way, in the next section.

Pay at the time, or pre-pay in advance? At first, it might seem frugal to have people pay for what they spend; let them pay for what it costs, when you know who ran up the cost. But in the case of birth and death, it's going to be 100%, and the amount of it is a lottery. By far the more important issue is the compound interest you earn by paying in advance. Using the rule of thumb that money at 7% will double in ten years, a life expectancy of 90 should double 9 times from birth to death. That is, a dollar at birth is worth $512 at death.

What's more, 50% of Medicare is reported to be spent in the last four years of someone's life. That's likely to represent terminal care, but it doesn't matter. If you prepay those four years, the rest of Medicare has its cost cut in half. In those two simple statements is found the nut of paying for half of Medicare for $100 -- ninety years from now. It's up to actuaries and accountants to find the "sweet spot", of the most revenue enhancement for the shortest time of investment.

Medicare Including Retirement, Pearl # 2

Invest the Withholding Tax and Pre-pay Medicare? Borrowing to pay for Medicare, except temporarily, has very little to be said for it. On the other hand, the choice between pre-paying for it and paying at the time of service, is a closer argument. Pre-payment can sometimes be arranged to reduce the price out of recognition of the interest foregone, but usually the seller gets the better of such a deal. In this section, we propose to arrange the payment stream to give the buyer the interest, but Medicare finances are so strained, it doesn't make a heavy impact. About a quarter of Medicare cost is paid from premiums from current beneficiaries. If that were collected in advance over a period of forty years like the payroll deduction, the combined interest payments would considerably reduce the eventual total cost. Unfortunately, young people are now so suspicious the money will be diverted to other purposes, it is a political question whether they would permit the withholding to be increased in amount. Furthermore, the other half of Medicare is essentially borrowed, so interest payments each way would about cancel each other without affecting the principle cost.

They would, however, probably be sufficient to keep the debt from continuing to rise at 7% a year, and that's a major advance. The withholding tax and the Medicare premiums would remain the same, the benefits would be unchanged. So what's in it for the average voter? Most accountants would say it was still a desirable change toward a more stable system, but many politicians would say it runs a risk without any political benefit at the next election. Everybody is correct; it isn't enough but it is something. It solves a definable portion of the problem, of bringing future deficit increases to a standstill. Things are so bad I'm afraid that's all you can buy for $3.5 billion a year. We must find some way to supplement it, but it's a start. We have five other suggestions:

Devise Some Way to Escrow Long-term Funding. New revenue ordinarily arrives as cash, and is invested in short-term loans until it is decided what to do with it. With thirty-day loans, or even overnight loans, you just have to wait a little, in order to restore cash status. But money market funds show us what can potentially happen. If customers get into a sudden panic, they want their money back immediately. If it's already invested in thirty-year mortgages, the money market fund may go bankrupt unless someone "bails them out". Which is to say, loans them more money to supply some cash -- even though they have ample funds frozen in long term investments. The creditors have their own creditors to consider. If no one will help out, the creditors may shut them down and you get the beginning of a liquidity crash.

Because of this remote but very real possibility, the longer the loan, the higher its interest rate, because the liquidity risk gets extended. That's bad if you are a borrower, but pleasant if you are a lender. Therefore, if the Medicare wage-tax receipts flowed into a frozen single-purpose investment account, creditors would be more assured money would be unrequested before the stated time, and its rate of return could rise with this new attractiveness. Just how much extra income would be provided is a little uncertain, because very few loans are currently for longer than thirty years. However, about forty-five years are potentially available between age 21 and 65, and educated guesses could be made. A one-or-two percent rise in income might change many calculations, not just this one alone.

Find Ways to Extend the Years at Compound Interest. Since retirement is conventional at age 65, a fund for retirement will immediately start to dwindle until the date of death. But many people continue to work, or have other retirement funding sources. If they do not need the surplus immediately, they should be permitted to leave it in the escrow fund, to prolong its term. This could be either fixed-term extensions or demand deposits, at the election of the depositor, and its election would make these funds preferable to retain, compared with Social Security, for example.

The open-endedness of retirement is always going to be a problem. If we speak in averages, they suggest half of the population will be dead, mid-way to the average. Any unexpended surplus after their deaths will be a source of contention, and there will be a struggle for it between heirs and longer-term survivors. If the compounding of unused income could continue longer, for even five years after death, the extra revenue would be considerable.

Continue to Earn Interest after the Death of the Depositor, as in a Trust Fund Long ago, a perpetuity was defined as one lifetime, plus 21 years. Adding another two decades would add two more doublings, and still not run afoul of inheritance traditions. In effect, it would increase the multiplier from 512 to one -- to 2048 to one, increasing the number of newborns who could afford $100, considerably, by making it only $25.

Because of the *de minimus* initial deposits, it would be a small matter to devote a small portion of the deposit to a backward-funding for childbirth costs. My Libertarian friends would be shocked to hear the proposal, but this small diversion would settle a myriad of cases before the Matrimonial courts about paternity, divorce, single parenthood and even same-sex marriage. Indeed, the financial incentive might be so great it would affect behavior, and need to be debated on that level separately.

But all of the foregoing is small-time, based on the mistaken notion the system is basically sound. Let's look, without pretense, for seriously larger amounts of money:

Contingency Fund. Any projection a century in advance risks making gross mistakes in its planning. No matter how confident the predicting party may seem, it is only prudent to have a contingency fund, when the multiplier of compound interest is so great. For example, most people can expect to be of Medicare age when they die, but not everyone will do so. But mostly a contingency will need to cover the considerable risk of simple miscalculation, without creating a temptation to divert it. The size of the contribution is scarcely a handicap. That is, a contingency fund of $2000 can be envisioned from the gift of $1 to a newborn. Since you know with absolute certainty that every newborn will die some day, a contingency fund of a million dollars per person is possible with a grant of $500 to everyone born in poverty, so long as you don't spend any of it for 111 years, providing you can get an average 7% return, and providing the government doesn't devise other uses for your money in the meantime.

Incidentally, increasing public resistance to inflation is one of the hidden virtues of this proposal. Most people would laugh at such a long-term projection. For a single individual, yes, for an extended family, not so much. The trick is to get started with small amounts, which don't attract much attention until they demonstrate some power.

Instead of fanciful extrapolations, it is possible to say almost every working person could summon up $200 per child, and the government could summon up $200 for those who can't. This is what is needed to provide supplements which would accomplish reasonable goals for lifetime healthcare, plus a somewhat more modest description of a comfortable retirement supplement to Social Security. And for those who are unable to support themselves for handicap reasons, the government might summon up the cost for indigents. In the long run, that would be a bargain investment. Since every child has two parents, it leaves a 100% cushion for under-estimates when we extend this idea to children. The problem is not arithmetic, it is public acceptance of the whole idea of individual long-term contingency funds, plus a way to store such a fund for centuries at a time, protecting it from pilfering by its custodians.

First and Last Years of Life Re-Insurance By far the best proposal for refinancing Medicare, however, is to anticipate the way science is going to re-design costs. In the long, long, run, there will be very little medical cost left, except the first and last years of life. We have no idea how long it will take, but that's the direction it is going.

So, phase in a re-structuring of funding for both children and elderly first, and then add in the rest of a lifespan, step by step. The rest of the lifespan will eventually shrink as a cost center, while the beginning and end would not. Be sure to do all this in such a way that maximizes investment income at compound interest. This might be a project under construction for decades, but its first step would be to begin funding for the Last Four Years of Life, which happens to be an early step in the proposal for refinancing Medicare. Since the reader may be unprepared for the topic, it is considered in a free-standing way, in the next section.

Pearl #3: Medicare Supplement, Only 20 Percent of a Pearl on the String

Now that we have described Health Savings Accounts as the string linking a string of pearls, we must have a second look at one of the pearls, because in a sense it is two of them. Medicare, it may be recalled, only pays for 80% of its patient's liability, while the other 20% is the patient responsibility. That is, Medicare has a 20% co-payment, which amounts to a 20% reduction in benefits. Most people who can afford it, will purchase a secondary insurance policy from Blue Cross or a commercial insurer, to cover this 20% liability, thus restoring the 20% of benefits at their own expense. Those who cannot afford such policies will often apply to state Medicaid, to become what is known in the trade as a "dual eligible". Those who are not eligible for Medicaid will often just take a chance on their personal resources, often becoming a source of the hospital's or doctors' bad debts. It is thus a curious feature that much of a hospital's bad debts come from the lower middle class.

Co-pay has a long history and a bad reputation. Most textbooks will classify it as a form of patient participation in his costs, and a restrainer of abusive claims. But it long ago developed the practical role of adjusting premium cost to available budget during group negotiations. If you don't get sick, you will have no co-pay obligations, but if you do get sick, it extinguishes 20% of the cost. So, although Medicare co-pay secondary insurance responds to the 20% co-pay feature of Medicare, in company negotiations for group policies for younger employees, it can be 30% or 27% or some other number, because the negotiators discovered that doing so reduced the cost of the insurance by 30% or 27% or whatever. It greatly facilitated middle-of-the night negotiations for the limits of coverage, with calculations on the back of an envelope, and probably had little relationship to restraining medical overuse. Quite obviously, it created the need for a secondary insurance, with a double dose of administrative costs and profits. So an expensive and largely futile feature has persisted for seventy or more years, deeply imbeded in Medicare for fifty. Usually the carrier for the secondary insurance is the administrator for the 80% which the government pays, but nevertheless two confusing reports ("explanation of benefits") for two different insurances come trickling in to the patient separately, two or three months after one treatment took place. But it does save the government 20% of its cost, so it persists. You will notice this 80/20 formula makes no effort to define or assign the extra insurance company costs and profits, which are negotiated privately. If utilization is affected little by co-pay, costs are nevertheless directly escalated by using two insurances to pay for a single medical encounter. Three insurances, if you include Major Medical policies.

In the case of Medicare, there is another quirk. As mentioned earlier, about 50% of the government's share of the cost, is borrowed. Insurance companies often borrow money, too, but usually not attached to a specific policy. While there may be hidden arrangements between Medicare and its secondary carriers, on the surface it would appear the secondary carrier's 20%, actually represents 33% of Medicare's cash flow. If that's the case, nothing short of a bull in the China shop will dislodge the preposterous dual-insurance system. Furthermore, it seems likely this cash leverage is playing an important hidden role in the ACA negotiations with large group employers. Eventually, this leverage is what might threaten ACA with disruption, but that particular issue gets us off the topic of Medicare, though the issues sound similar.

Having earlier reviewed the finances of the 80% of Medicare, and found that financing it is rather precarious, let's look at the more modest goal of financing the 20% co-payment insurance with the available resources. That's a more modest goal, and a more achievable one, one which would at least remove a large source of public confusion and dissatisfaction. It might, for example, explain why it takes weeks or months for a computerized "explanation of benefits" to appear at the patient's home, after he has long since forgotten the charges it matches.

The main purpose of eliminating the Medicare co-pay feature is to eliminate the extra cost of a second insurance administration. Once you grasp the unlikelihood that a copayment would affect utilization if you only feel its impact after you go home from the hospital, you see the argument that it does not affect inpatient behavior. Outpatient costs might be another matter, although even that has not been demonstrated, and the alternate use of debit cards by Health Savings Accounts seems to point in the other direction (see page 9). The conclusion would have to be that you have two choices: reduce the duplication of insurance companies, or reduce the duplication of policies. Just exactly which approach would save most money, requires greater access to the data, and more expert analysis. Superficially, it seems likely the outpatient use is greater among younger people, resulting in a greater saving after compound interest is applied. A change of this magnitude requires more investigation than nonprofessional outsiders are likely to provide.

Nevertheless, eliminating the copay in some manner would provide a leveraged advantage. The extraction of the cost of the last four years of life would cut Medicare direct costs by 50%, and the elimination of copay would reduce it further. This is an example of the sort of leveraged cost reduction we have in mind. Migration of the center of medical care, from the hospital to the suburban retirement village would be another.

If we were commercial insurance investors dealing with a failing health insurance partner, no additional money infusions would seem sensible until Medicare stopped losing so much money. Because we are talking about a government program however, we must resort to the stance that a new program does not have to accept old debts, only new ones that it had a hand in creating. Therefore, this proposal does not include the repayment of old debts, regarding them as the government's problem to resolve. In many ways, Medicare was a noble achievement, but even the richest country in the world cannot afford to run a 50% deficit indefinitely, in an entitlement program grown so large. Undertaking to correct its mistakes does not imply assuming its debts. Furthermore looking forward, a looming retirement funding crisis, of at least equal size, threatens to replace it as the largest consequence of its heedlessness. Was this lengthening of longevity by thirty years a bad thing? Of course not. The bad thing was to let finances get into their present state before addressing them. The bad thing was to kick the can down the road, for fifty years. Because so few people seem to understand them, let's next review a quick summary of Medicare finances.

The Basic Funding Structure of Medicare. Approximately one quarter of Medicare is paid for by its **premiums**, often derived from reduced Social Security payments, (a circular solution, if you regard prolonged longevity as a hidden cost of Medicare). Another quarter of Medicare is paid for by a 3% **payroll withholding tax** on younger, working people. (Unfortunately, this money is immediately spent, in a process quaintly known as "pay as you go"). And finally, half of Medicare expense ($260 billion annually) isn't paid for at all, it›s just **debt,**initially laundered into general taxation and then floated away by bond issues.

Suggested Solutions:

1. Extract Income From the Float. To attack the problem we would probably need to do many complicated things, but the first step might be pretty simple. We once contemplated a transfer-entrant into this revised program be required to sign an authorization to **redirect payments for Medicare cost on his behalf to his own Health Savings Account**. (Incidentally, it might also include an accounting of copayments and subsidies.) From the beneficiary's point of view, nothing changes except the postal address of his payments, which becomes his Health Savings Account. If he is between the age of 25 and 65, his withholding tax is so directed; if he is already on Medicare, it is his Medicare premiums. That's a payment stream which stretches sixty years, overall. Depending on his present age, first it is one, and eventually it is the other. That wasn't so hard, was it?

The money now starts to earn investment income, which is new money for the program, with the surplus eventually going through the Health (and Retirement) Savings Account into retirement funds. One way of looking at this rearrangement is to say the beneficiary has been given the money to pay his bills, but relieved of the obligation to pay old debts. He has also been given extra latitude to invest the income and use the profit to fund his retirement. What does the government get out of it? It potentially gets an abatement to annual increases in debt, plus the hope the retirement incentive will restrain cost escalation. If you wish, you could say the principal value to the government is creating the incentive at the end of this and other programs which join the string of pearls. Meanwhile both parties can pray that science will reduce future medical costs, not raise them. But however it turns out, this solution unfortunately does turn out to be too small to make a significant change in the management of Medicare's debt, so we go on to other approaches. However, it raises an interesting point for a brief digression:

Using the shorthand that Health Savings Accounts ought to produce at least a 7% return, and money at 7% doubles in ten years, a quick look at pre-financing present Medicare payments overall is a little disappointing. In the Secretary's report, Mrs. Sibelius tells us annual Medicare expenses are about $560 billion, and cash revenue aims to be half that, or $280 billion. If the cash revenue only resided in the individuals' HSAs, it might add 7% revenue, or 19.6 billion per year. That sounds like a worth-while amount, and it could be approximated it would apply to each yearly age cohort for 65 years (45 years of wage withholding, followed by 20 years of Medicare premiums). Since the system has been in place for many years, it has reached a steady state, net of demographic and economic variations. So an age cohort would collect a lifetime average of 65 x 19.6, or $1,274 billion, or 1274 divided by 500 million individual recipients, or $2548 per lifetime. It certainly sounds as if the maneuver would be worthwhile, because the government would be no worse off, and the subscriber would have $2548 more in his HSA.

But Michigan Blue Cross has estimated the average person spends $350,000 per lifetime for health, half of which is covered by Medicare; and so 25% of that is Medicare revenue. Even by the roughest sort of estimation, this proposed re-direction of revenue would save less than 1% of the cost of Medicare, because revenue is such a small part of cost. To put it another way, this approach might be an important funding device if indebtedness were not such a large part of Medicare's budget. We have not calculated the effect of compounding, which might theoretically reach several times its original size as stated revenue.. On the other hand, neither have we recognized the annual increase in Medicare spending, which its trustees report to be 5.7% per year. Both 7% and

5.7% are fragile projections of the future, one of Medicare spending and the other of the stock market. As long as annual increases in cost are so close to investment revenue from cash revenue, any hope of substantial investment revenue is at the mercy of minor yearly volatility. and cannot be relied on. The best to be reasonably hoped for this proposal is to stop the growth of Medicare deficits. It should be done, nonetheless, but there is no great political advantage to be gained from emerging with the problem apparently unchanged.

A second weakness of this approach is variation in proportionality between revenue and expenses among various government programs. Last year, the Social Security budget was $888 billion, while the total Medicare budget was $618. A quick glance at my secretary's pay stub reveals she has five times as much withheld for Social Security as for Medicare. The approach of investing the withholdings until the day they are spent is a good one. But if widely applied, would have drastically unexpected consequences unless other things are changed.

Additional Proposals to Supplement Medicare Income. Since Medicare is so underfunded by its revenue, the hope of extracting additional income above 7% is pretty dim. Therefore, the hope of significant cost abatement must come from three other proposals, all of which require the investment of fresh funding. That is, they are investments, not miracles:

2. The Second J-Shaped Curve, Within Medicare. All healthcare costs with the exception of premature birth, genetic disorders and the like, are migrating to older age groups. One of the main sources of disruption is the migration of costly illness from working people to people on Medicare.

But even within Medicare, costs are also migrating into later life. Half of Medicare costs are paid on behalf of the last four years of someone's life. Since Medicare extends about twenty years after retirement, half of total Medicare cost would vanish from its annual budget as a result of placing this burden somewhere else. This might be called the Last Four Years of Life Reinsurance, a component of the First and Last Years of Life reconstruction of healthcare finance, to be described later.

The consequence is partly funding forward toward death, partly funding backward toward childbirth, and so reducing the transition time. The present system, it may be recalled, always funds forward toward death, and buries childhood in "family" plans. That's the background.

But death is the end of the line; costs can't get pushed any later, although curiously, revenue just might be. Therefore, the unique features for transitioning Medicare to some other system reside not only in the universality, but also the finality of the cost of terminal care. This entity has a soft lower border, but we know that half of Medicare costs are concentrated in the last four years of life, creating a simple surrogate, although not a pure one. Paying this version of terminal cost separately allows the remaining cost of Medicare to be cut in half, by spreading it over the remaining sixteen years. Transition time is also halfed. Moreover, smaller pieces are considerably easier to fit into a transition scheme, so the ultimate product fits the cost curve more comfortably. By the way, the last years of life are not the same as the last years of Medicare, and can only be calculated in retrospect, after the death of the individual.. This is the reality which allows one insurance to be paid out as costs are incurred, and a second, a re-insurance, to repay the first one after the facts are in. Funding the re-insurance from birth allows compound interest to pay for most of the magic in a forward direction. And making obstetrics/pediatrics into a gift from parent to child, allows it to fund backward. Now, we are beginning to approach the way Nature makes us pay our bills.

3. Contingency Fund. But wherever is this money, half the cost of Medicare, to come from? Terminal care is predictable the day you are born, so you might as well fund it when it is cheap. A separate fund could be imagined, but for simplicity we lump terminal care financing into a general contingency fund. So we next propose to complete the Medicare revenue issue by adding a contingency fund, essentially substituting a subsidy of $1 at birth for a deficit sixty times as large at age 65, and depending on compound interest to make up the difference. (It may well require about $100 up front, but less if we extended its duration by two or three decades.) How fast it would actually grow in the intervening 65 years would become evident before then, and appropriate adjustments made, but the person or agency to make the decision should be specified with care. The sixty to one estimate comes from 7% doubling principal every ten years, 2,4,8, 16, 32, 64 doublings in sixty years. How much to begin with is actually the last calculation, adjusted to balance the books as experience gathers to improve the estimate, and adjustment applied to its duration.

4. Extended Contingency Fund. The contingency fund ending when Medicare begins might anyway generate a 64 to one magnification of the initial deposit. However, it could extend to 250-to-one if its boundary were the day of average death (now 84) or 1000 to one if it added 21 years to the date of death and ended where the common law now says a perpetuity begins (one lifetime plus 21 years). Innovations of this sort make many people squirm, but the underfinancing of Medicare in the past leaves little opportunity for conventionality in the future. All of this magic is a function of the mathematics of compound interest; objections to it are sociological, not mathematical. With a leverage of 1000 to one, it is difficult to imagine an inability to pay the front-end $100, when $100,000 is so far in excess of what actually seems needed.

Sweeping proposals of this sort however, do tend to dump their problems at the far end, so the ultimate goal is best stated to be <u>funding part of the individual system backward to childbirth, partly forward to death, and still having a contingency fund for safety</u>. That is, the system as a whole may be volatile and require internal borrowing, but each individual HRSA ends up with balanced books. By implication rather than calculation, in ninety or so years, you get rid of the Medicare debt. That's approximately how long it took to create it, too. The system does not "cover" retirement, except perhaps for bare-bones Social Security. It merely closes the individual books after death as described in other sections. Last-Year Coverage is also designed to save money, and thus eventually to generate some funds for retirement, but not likely at first. First and Last Year <u>re-insurance</u> is intended to resemble an accordion, quickly going to the first 25 years of life and the last 4 years of life, then slowly adding other years in the middle. Somewhere along the line, it might even shrink somewhat. At the moment, it appears terminal illness usually lasts four years, a process which might be thought of as "breaking the cocoon of health". Half of Medicare expenditure occurs in the last four years of life, leaving quite a surplus when the other sixteen years of cost are redistributed. In any event, the "accordion" effect is available for use in the transitions.

This completes our proposal for refinancing Medicare. The first step is to eliminaate the supplemental copayment burden by substituting pre-payment for the 20% revenue, and meanwhile letting small front-end investments grow to appreciable size for the remaining 80%. Until we see what must be done to integrate the ACA with the rest of health-care, it's likely to use up our political capital with the public, just to make that start. Secondly and later, it reduces itself to stabilizing cost increases by first investing the float created by the J-shaped cost curve, combined with cutting forward-financing loose from the debts of the past. Even a program allowed to concentrate on its 50% forward short-fall, must employ some novel approaches to produce annually $250-300 billion in either cost cuts or new revenue. We suggest compound interest is entirely capable of achieving it mathematically by making a total stock market investment starting at birth and continuing to death, or even 21 years after death. All that is necessary to do it on paper is to invest sufficient money at first. Unfortunately, there is an invisible limit to how much the populace is willing to tolerate as an investment, even on such bargain-basement terms, which I postulate to be about $500 per newborn child. Will that suffice for a 65-year investment? Possibly. Will a hundred-year investment cover it? Almost certainly. Do we as a nation have the patience for a hundred-year investment, or the degree of honesty in our agents to leave such huge amounts un-pilfered for a century? That's far less certain.

How Would This Combined Approach Make Medicare Solvent?
Medicare has become so over-extended that conventional approaches are soon exhausted. Like any other proposal that might work, this one relies on approaches which are usually best avoided. First of all, it depends on such long time periods that unexpected events would be the rule, not the exception. Many Congresses of many political parties would have to understand it and leave it unharmed for a century. Secondly, such huge amounts of money are involved that tampering, embezzling and fraud are not merely possible, but inevitable. These two problems would confront any reformer. From these two

39

obstacles emerges a third one. Individual Health Accounts would have less risk than gigantic single payers, because some people will be stupid, reckless and venal. If you make up your mind in advance that you will rescue everyone who doesn't succeed, the whole system will be no better than a single gigantic reinsurer overseen by either an idiot or a crook. The opportunities for illegal gains will exceed the opportunities for honest managers. Therefore, smaller is better than bigger, simpler is better than complicated, and success is never guaranteed.

Medicare, possibly fundable, retirement income, probably not. To do the quick math in your head, it is useful to remember money at 7% doubles in 10 years. The Medicare deficit doubles every fourteen years. Since Medicare revenue is half of its expenses, its revenue invested at 7% would generate 3.5% of expenses, or just about enough to cancel out the annual rise in the deficit. Current interest rates do not achieve that, but current rates seldom do. During the eight years of the Obama administration, low-cost total market indices averaged 11% gain. Much of this never reached the average stockholder because the finance industry absorbed it, but things seem to be changing quickly. The pharmaceutical industry may possibly be over-represented in the index, but we are proposing to make the average patient become an average stockholder. Let's take the four components:

#1. The Contingency Fund. is designed to be overfunded for contingencies, so it is hard to say how much it should be. The most conservative investment period would terminate at death, but expand to whatever age is necessary, up to age 105. That means the $500 initial deposit never varies. Congress might however, decide to vary the initial deposit to use a shorter time period. It makes no mathematical difference, but its political difference might be considerable.

#2. Delay Liquidating the HRSA at death. Although things get a little threadbare beyond this point, there is no reason to hold back borrowing for a purpose. We are at the point in the compound interest curve where holding the funds for ten years after death would multiply the original subsidy by 128 instead of 64. We are paying the Chinese much less than that for the Treasury bonds, and they would probably be greatly relieved to see a way of recovering their investment. It may not sit very well with some people, but it would surely guarantee repayment. At the moment, repayment looks rather doubtful.

#3. Investing the Pay as You Go. The problems created for others in the payment process have to be reckoned with. We propose the individuals continue pay/go temporarily for half of the withholding tax receipts, effectively unchanged because half the cost has been transferred but the withholding tax revenue remains constant. What is essentially involved is to balance the problems of the current budget staff against the problems of passing acceptable legislation. But once more, the mathematical "sweet spot" is comparatively easy to calculate, but the political effects are more intangible. It is probably impossible for an outsider to have a firm opinion.

Additional unknowns in this equation are how much nursing home costs from state Medicaid plans would eventually emerge as Medicare deficits. It is common knowledge that although custodial costs are not allowable costs, states have found ways to make them a federal responsibility. We also understand the HRSA owner may get less than 7% income on his deposits. Although the Chinese debt would stop rising, past indebtedness remains unpaid. Current Medicare bills would have to be paid for probably another decade, and may well rise in size. Ultimately, the way to balance the books is to raise the contributions. So, privatizing Medicare might or might not make it costless, but would greatly relieve its present costs. Funding of past debts will have to come from other sources. However, contributions from the two contingency funds could easily be increased.

Is medical finance really so complicated most people couldn't handle it by themselves?

#4. The Last Four Years of Life Half of Medicare costs appear in the last four years of Life. By reimbursing Medicare for the last four years from other sources, Medicare's average cost is cut in half. but the withholding tax remains the same. Therefore, we come closer to breaking even in several decades, although we probably won't quite make it.

#5. Simplicity, Simplicity. To begin with the opposite of simplicity, two quite unacceptable new ways to manage the medical payment system suggest themselves. One alternative is to **consolidate the whole**

41

industry, with one corporate administrative arm assuming the payment tasks for everybody, along with the whole delivery system. That scarcely seems appropriate management for a health complex which is already too big to manage. But it seems to generate many current proposals, especially those coming from the bureaucracy itself. Another idea, based on its resemblance to whole-life insurance, proposes **a giant company or government department to concentrate on health finance**, doing it for everybody. It might seem suitable for an insurance company, a medical school, a computer company, or a medical society. That seems to be what these organizations would like, but it immediately creates additional complexity, because computers only work if you specify some response to every contingency in advance. In a sense, this version of "Single Payer" would be a throw-back to the days when only a big company or a big government could afford to own a computer.

If you want a simple system, give it to individuals who have an incentive to keep it simple.

Is medical finance really so complicated most people couldn't handle it by themselves? Let's remember the anguished words of the Tzar: "I don't run Russia. Ten thousand clerks run Russia." What the Tsar was saying, was the problem isn't individual complexity, the problem is the huge volume of simple problems. For example, if we proposed to butter everybody's bread, it wouldn't be hard to do, it would be hard to manage.

Transfer Slips, and Monthly statements, Only. So, yes and no to computers, which what all this amounts to. Abundant cheap computers tempt us to use them for simple tasks, at the risk of making the simple task complex. (In another generation, self-correcting code may correct this problem, at the same time it widens the opportunity for vandals.) The proposal made here instead is a confederation of otherwise free-standing organizations (The Pearls), hiring their own experts, feeding into a common channel of Health Savings Accounts owned by individual patients (The String). Individuals could hire consultants if they pleased but the decisions should be so simple the average high school graduate could cope with them.

One standardized lifetime account form, which serves as a transfer system for a single person's various bal-

ances. Sort of like a check-book. It provides a common incentive to be frugal for future retirement, and a common way to multiply such savings.

If that won't suffice for some tasks, we are travelling down the same path as the income tax, and should re-consider such high-handedness.

There might be many networks, as long as their balances are uniformly transferable and they each link ultimately to a transferable retirement fund (The Goal) and a transferable investment fund (The Multiplier). Such networks might grow very large, but still remain quite simple, and decisions which belong to the patient would remain within his control. The only outward purpose of such paperwork would be to transfer credits of the owner to debits of the same owner or vice versa, with the adjusted balance ultimately coming to rest in his retirement account, creating a common incentive to be medically frugal. They would maintain adequate records (which mostly no one ever reads), an information source, and a designated HSA representative, but their outward form and purpose would remain recording a transfer slip. If you want a simple system, give it to individuals who have an incentive to keep it simple. Don't give it to people who have an incentive to make it complicated.

This particular feature has a political element. The American public now imagines it gets a bargain with Medicare, somehow getting a dollar of healthcare for fifty cents, and therefore a treasure they are unwilling to surrender. In all probability, no organization except the government could function long with such a deficit, so taking the deficit away from the government necessarily places it in the hands of someone who must balance his books. Somehow, legal protections for the patients against the debts of organizations which participate in the confederation must be established, so they can occasionally provide benefits at a loss, but only within stated limits. Called a "loss leader", the situation is a common one. Two additional savings multipliers must be added, although they will be explained shortly, along with two important investment designs. There are four large sources of new revenue within Medicare:

Investment Mechanisms. We promised to discuss two investment mechanisms which might help matters. The first is the tendency of compound interest to rise with time. We have already shown above that adding another decade to the example will have an exaggerated effect on the outcome. This is an inherent quality of compound interest which crept up on us as science has conquered early death, and should have wide application in the future. As we learn how to avoid borrowing and learn how to be successful creditors, it should become a commonplace to rearrange financing to optimize it.

The second new model is **index investing.** As international borrowing has vastly increased the money supply, interest rates seem to have settled at a new low. Bonds have always been a zero-sum investment, but recent trends seem to set an even lower boundary. Common stock has more risk and volatility, but John Bogle and others have shown that it is practically useless for an ordinary person to buy anything but total-market common-stock index funds, since the fees charged by intermediaries wipe out any profit from active investing. We recommend a heavy emphasis on this method. Beyond that basic approach, other strategies may be considered as a way to add fractions of a percent to total returns, best avoided by people without experience, or lifetime years to recover from investment misjudgments.

In Final Summary of Privatizing Medicare. Even with considerable twisting, Medicare is so underfunded, no way can be found to self-fund it without adding two to five hundred dollars per person as a pump-primer, adjusted for being added at birth. That's a great bargain, or course, but it will meet far more resistance than five hundred dollars is worth, mostly centered on the long transition time. Even with tinkering, it would require forty or fifty years at the most optimistic. In the Pearls on a String concept, the deficit might be made up by surplus generated by other programs, but it is unlikely to be able to identify such a cross-investor. The Affordable Care Act does not look as though it is going to generate a surplus, for example. In the long run, further privatization of the IPO variety seems the only way to shorten the transition time to the point where the public would accept waiting so long. Nevertheless, although complete resolution of the problem is probably presently impossible, there is no reason why partial solutions would not help.

Re-funding Medicare, Pearl #2, Part 3

So we end up funding Medicare mathematically, but with misgivings about both the politics and the economics of it. It would not be the first time America launched an adventure without the money to finance it, as we do almost every time we start a war, or face a depression. However, both the ACA is in doubt, and linked with it is the idea of a single payer with Medicare as a model. Although I have grave misgivings about consolidating delivery systems as a first step, it could be a decision that is beyond the suggestion of a citizen.

Under the present uncertain circumstances -- of wishing to put the ideas forward but lacking the ability to control the environment -- it seems better to hold back on grander designs than just saving a little money. The linkage of Medicare and its secondary insurance is both tight and of long standing. By just eliminating the second insurance policy, we might eliminate a large and useless expense as well as suggest a few ways to save more. Isn't saving several billion dollars worth some effort? The factors which would lead America to embark on a financial crusade as radical as suggested here, are not to be found in mathematics, or even in one-man logic. They are cultural and emotional, mostly evolving out of endless simplification and repetition. The public might be persuaded to try something on 20%, which they would be afraid to try out on a whole program, however floundering it might appear to be.

How Would This Particular Approach Make Medicare Solvent? It wouldn't, but it would help. And it would provide a demonstration of the practicality of some of these ideas for worthy motives, and still leave room to back down if they unexpectedly fail. Most people do not trust their own judgment of complicated math, so we have made it simple. It is surely not the case that every single solution is either too complicated to understand, or too simple to be believable. Every grand proposal, from Otto von Bismarck's social security through the European systems, to Blue Cross/Blue Shield, followed by Harry

Truman, Hillary Clinton's foray into HMO, to Barrack Obama's ACA, has proved to be overambitious at the beginning, and woefully inadequate at the end. It seems there ought to be better ways to do things, but this is our way.

Medicare's original design has become so over-extended it has exhausted conventional insolvency approaches. Like any other proposal that might work, our own plan relies on approaches which are usually thought to be best avoided. So the first fundamental is to keep the core of it simple, and be willing to discard the embellishments if circumstances undermine them. The doctors should devise the medical choices, the patients must control the finances, paying only for what pleases them. Government has a limited role in market failures, but very little role in defining them. The goal is to eliminate disease, ultimately reducing its cost to a framework of the first year of life and the last year of life. Anything more must defend itself against efforts to improve, then eliminate it.

And there is another idea which needs testing. Alexander Hamilton persuaded George Washington that "A national debt, if it be not too large, is a national treasure." In 2006, we may have discovered what is a little too large to be sustainable, by permitting banks to convert mortgage debt to stockholder equity and then watching banks topple over from the sudden shift. Up to that time, it was quite legal to rebalance excess debt that way, which is why no one has gone to jail for doing it. And now we have the uncertainty over whether to encourage more of it (as a safety valve), or punish it (as toppling over the entire economy). It does not help matters for the two political parties to take extreme positions without more evidence. Pre-paying for medical care instead of borrowing to pay for it, is an indirect way of testing this thesis.

First of all, our own proposal depends on such long time periods that unexpected events could be the rule, not the exception. Nevertheless, many Congresses of many political parties would have to understand the basics and leave them unharmed for a century. Secondly, such huge amounts of money are involved that tampering, embezzling and fraud are not merely possible, but inevitable. These problems would confront any reformer. From them emerges a third one. Multitudes of individual

Health Accounts would have less risk overall than gigantic single payers, because small ones can only be converted into bigger ones, not defeated in a single pitched battle. Inevitably some individuals in charge of any system will prove to be stupid, reckless and venal. The real question is: Compared with What? If you make up your mind in advance that you will rescue everyone who doesn't succeed, the whole system will be no better than a single gigantic reinsurer overseen by either an idiot or a crook, and probably both, from time to time. Index investing is itself a triumph of everyman against the experts, after all. For long periods, single payer systems may be run by saints, but diversity is more resilient in the long run. The more important issue is to define how you will respond when you detect "imperfect agency". The opportunities for illegal gains will inevitably exceed the individual opportunities for honest managers, in size if not in frequency. Therefore, smaller decision units are better than bigger, simpler is better than complicated, and success should never be guaranteed. The irony of the role reversal between the political party of individualism and the party of diversity, is not to be overlooked.

Medicare financing could possibly be eventually covered by this approach, retirement income financing, probably not. To do the quick math in your head, it is useful to remember money at 7% doubles in 10 years. Current interest rates do not achieve that, but then current rates seldom do. During the eight years of the Obama administration, low-cost total market index averaged 11% gain. Most people would never have guessed that outcome in advance. Much of it never reached the average stockholder because the government (taxes and inflation) and the finance industry absorbed it, but public restlessness may change things. The pharmaceutical industry may possibly be over-compensated, but that's not necessarily permanent, either. In this proposal we are proposing to make the average patient become an average stockholder, with little voice in management perhaps, but ultimate ability "to talk with his feet", to buy and sell. Let's take the six components of the proposal:

#1. The co-pay feature. We've offered our opinion that co-pay has little restraining effect on spending, and is only a device for adjusting the amount of insurance to the buyer's budget. So let's take it as that, and use the amount of the copay as, not 20%, but whatever fits our budget. We advocate the accordion principle for predicting future revenue uncertainty. Furthermore, we would abandon the pretense that it is a second insurance policy, and simply pay the carriers a fee for administrative help in running Medicare. That opens it to a bidding process related to work actually performed, eliminates the State insurance commissioner as an actor in this drama, and eliminates a huge source of confusion with the public. Imagine, one statement of benefits instead of two.

#2. The Contingency Fund. is designed to be overfunded for contingencies, so it is hard to say what its upper limit should be. And although on paper no one gets paid off for ninety years, banks are accustomed to rearranging the terms of a loan to shorten the time period for a fee. Dealing with transition periods is an old story for Congressional staff, since otherwise nothing would ever be upgraded. The most conservative investment period would terminate at death, but expand to whatever age is necessary to pay it off, up to age 105. That implies the initial deposit never varies. Congress might, however, decide to vary the initial deposit but devise a shorter fixed time period. It makes no mathematical difference, but its political difference might be considerable and we do not propose to weaken our case by getting into such weedy details.

Eventually, a "sweet spot" should emerge. But let's not drop the argument with a confession of modesty. An officer of a large paycheck company recently declared to me the revenues of essentially all government programs have nothing to do with expenses, and everything to do with politics. True, we operate under a general mandate to balance new appropriations with new revenue sources. But the current payroll deduction for Social Security is five times as high as the deduction for Medicare, with only about 25% difference in expenses between the two programs, for example. The accounting rules for appropriations could be made considerably less political without significant impairment of flexibility. In the long run it is not good politics for the public to discover you have been doing outrageous things. Over and over, you discover the Constitution is a cultural document, intolerant of judges who are obtuse.

#3. Delay Liquidating the HRSA at death. Although things get a little threadbare beyond this point, there is no reason to hold back borrowing for observed volatility. We are at the point in the compound interest curve, where holding the funds for ten years after death would multiply the original subsidy by 128 instead of 64; even 256 is conceivable. We are paying the Chinese much less than that for the Treasury bonds, and they would probably be relieved to see a way of recovering their investment. #2 may not sit very well with some people, but it would surely guarantee repayment, which at the moment, looks rather chancy.

#4. Investing the Pay as You Go. The problems created for others in the payment process have to be reckoned with. We propose the individuals continue pay/go temporarily for half of the withholding tax receipts. That's effectively unchanged because half the cost has been transferred, but the withholding tax revenue remains constant. What is essentially involved is to balance the problems of the current administrative staff against the problems of passing acceptable legislation. But once more, the mathematical "sweet spot" is comparatively easy to calculate, but the political effects are more intangible. It is probably impossible for an outsider to have a firm opinion.

Additional unknowns in this equation are how much nursing home costs from state Medicaid plans would eventually emerge in the form of Medicare deficits. It is common knowledge that although custodial costs are not allowable costs, states have found ways to make them a federal responsibility. We also understand the HRSA owner might get less than 7% income on his deposits. Although the Chinese debt would stop rising, past indebtedness remains unpaid. Current Medicare bills would have to be paid for probably another decade, and may well rise in size. Ultimately, the way to balance the books is to raise the contributions. So, privatizing Medicare might or might not make it costless, but would greatly relieve its present costs. Funding of retirements will have to come from other sources. However, right now contributions from the two contingency funds could easily be increased.

#4. The Last Four Years of Life Half of Medicare costs appear in the last four years of Life. By reimbursing Medicare for the last four years from other sources, Medicare's average cost is cut in half. but the withholding tax remains the same. Therefore, we come closer to breaking even in several decades, although we still probably won't quite make it. The essential feature of carving off terminal care is that it is half the cost of Medicare, and therefore reduces the burden on the other contrivances to reach the final goal of financing it.

#5. Simplicity, Simplicity. To begin with the opposite of simplicity, two quite unacceptable new ways to manage the medical payment system have been suggested by others. One alternative is to **consolidate the whole industry,** with one corporate administrative arm assuming the payment tasks for everybody, along with the whole delivery system. That scarcely seems appropriate management for a health complex which is already too big to manage. But it seems to generate many current proposals, especially those coming from the bureaucracy itself. Another idea, based on its resemblance to whole-life insurance, proposes **a giant company or government department to concentrate on health finance**, doing it for everybody. It might seem suitable for an insurance company, a medical school, a computer company, or a medical society. That seems to be what these organizations would like, but it immediately creates additional complexity, because computers only work if you specify some response to every contingency in advance. In a sense, this version of "Single Payer" would be a throw-back in thinking to the days when only a big company or a big government could afford to own a computer.

Is medical finance really so complicated most people couldn't handle it by themselves? Let's remember the anguished words Tzar Nicholas: "I don't run Russia. Ten thousand clerks run Russia." What the Tsar was saying, was the problem isn't individual complexity, the problem is the huge volume of simple problems. For example, if we proposed to butter everybody's bread, it wouldn't be hard to do, it would be hard to manage.

> Is medical finance really so complicated most people couldn't handle it by themselves?

#6. Linking the New Medicare with Health Savings Accounts.. Probably the most important feature of putting pearls on the string, is to avoid tangling the string for the convenience of the pearl. The purposes of the linkage are to acquire a connection to the retirement feature and its incentives to save, and to lengthen the time period of any compound interest. It is not to generate inter-plan borrowings or conveniences, particularly for the early entrants to the string of pearls, at the expense of the later ones.

For Health and Retirement Savings Accounts --- Transfer Slips, and Monthly statements, Only. So, yes and no to computers, which is what all this amounts to. Abundant cheap computers tempt us to use them for simple tasks, at the risk of making the simple task complex and losing the truth in a huge pile of statistics. (In another generation, self-correcting code may conquer this problem, at the same time it will widen the opportunity for vandals.)

The proposal made here instead, is a confederation of otherwise free-standing organizations (The Pearls), each hiring its own experts, feeding into a common channel of Health Savings Accounts owned by individual patients (The String). Individuals could hire consultants if they pleased but the decisions should be so simple the average high school graduate could cope with them.

One consolidated lifetime account form, which serves as a transfer vehicle for a single person's various balances. Sort of like a lifetime check-book. It provides a common incentive to be frugal for future retirement, and a common way to multiply such savings.

If that won't suffice for some tasks, we are travelling down the same path as the income tax, and should re-consider such high-handed laziness.

There might be many networks, as long as their balances are uniformly transferable and they each link ultimately to a transferable retirement fund (The Goal) and a transferable investment fund (The Multiplier). Such networks might grow very large, but still remain quite simple, and decisions which belong to the patient would remain within his control. The only outward purpose of such paperwork would be to transfer credits of the owner, to debits of the same owner or vice versa,

If you want a simple system, give it to individuals who have an incentive to keep it simple.

with the adjusted balance ultimately coming to rest in his *retirement account, creating a common incentive to be medically frugal.* This would maintain adequate "records" (which mostly no one ever reads), an information source, and a designated HSA representative, but their outward form and unit would remain a transfer slip. You are striving for a good retrieval system, not a good archive system. If you want a simple system, give it to individuals who have an incentive to keep it simple. Don't give it to people who have a graduate degree an incentive to make it complicated.

This particular feature has a political element. The American public now imagines it gets a bargain with Medicare, somehow getting a dollar of healthcare for fifty cents, and therefore a treasure they are unwilling to surrender. In all probability, no organization except the government could function long with such a deficit, so taking the deficit away from the government necessarily places it in the hands of someone who must balance his books. Somehow, legal protections for the patients against the debts of organizations which participate in the confederation must be established, so they can occasionally provide benefits at a loss, but only within stated limits. Called a "loss leader", the situation is a common one, but the effect is quite different from making the government a payer of last resort. Two additional savings multipliers must be added, although they will be explained shortly, along with two important investment designs.

Investment Mechanisms. We promised to discuss two investment mechanisms which might help matters. The first is the tendency of compound interest to rise with time. We have already shown above that adding another decade to the example will have an exaggerated effect on the outcome. This is an inherent quality of compound interest which crept up on us as science has conquered early death, and should have wide application in the future. As we learn how to avoid borrowing and learn how to be successful creditors, it should become a commonplace to rearrange financing to optimize it.

The second new model is **index investing.** As international borrowing has vastly increased the money supply, interest rates seem to have settled at a new low. Bonds have always been a zero-sum investment, but recent trends seem to set an even lower boundary. Common stock has more risk and volatility, but John Bogle and others have shown that it is practically useless for an ordinary person to buy anything but low cost total-market common-stock index funds ("passive investing"), since the fees charged by intermediaries tend to wipe out the profit from active investing. We recommend a heavy emphasis on this method. Beyond that basic approach, other strategies may be considered as a way to add fractions of a percent to total returns, but best avoided by people without experience, or lifetime years to recover from investment misjudgments.

In Final Summary of Privatizing Medicare. The public sector has been allowed to turn "privatization" into a term of contempt, when in fact it is a goal for the public sector to emulate. Very few people begin their careers in the public sector without spending their whole career there. In that sense, they are natural monopolists and act like them. We should strive for more varied career paths.

Even with considerable twisting, Medicare is so underfunded, no way can be found to self-fund it without adding several hundred dollars per person as a pump-primer. Of course, that's a great bargain compared with a hundred thousand dollars of medical care later on, but it will meet far more resistance than five hundred dollars is worth. Even then, it might require forty or fifty years at the most optimistic, to show a profit. In the Pearls on a String concept, the deficit might be made up by surplus generated by other programs, but Congress is unlikely to be willing to identify such a donor, and indeed it is a slippery path. The Affordable Care Act does not look as though it is going to generate a surplus, for example.

Transition to Revised Medicare: Pearl #2, Part 4

Transitions to new programs from old ones, are usually difficult. Transition from a post-paid system of Medicare to a pre-paid one is no different; but the huge size of the program makes it harder, deficit spending of the past fifty years makes it worse. Congress tends to act a little like Queen Victoria, outlining what it wants to achieve, and leaving the details up to the professionals on the Congressional staff, or the regulations applied by the Executive branch. The following are therefore only suggestions.

Up to this point, we have alluded to the possibility of a "last four years of life" concentration of expenses creating ample decades for compound interest to accumulate on savings, before the savings are later needed to reimburse Medicare for them. However, some people will die within the immediate next year after enactment, so some expenses will surely begin immediately. (That would be awkward, so it might be better to begin after a delay, starting with a cushion of the accumulated revenue; but temporary deficit spending, partial yearly payments, and a trailing transition fund are all alternative possibilities.)

The revenue for the early years would probably best come from absorbing the 20% co-insurance premiums, as the useless co-insurance is wound down. Since the last four years are said to contain half of the costs, they could be approximately matched to about 6% of the annual co-payment revenue (3% of annual Medicare cost) during the first fifteen years of Medicare, and declining amounts until the copayment is completely absorbed. That leaves a small shortfall for the copayment fund, which would in turn be compensated by either the contingency fund or Medicare premiums, recognizing that increases in Medicare debt would be stabilized by investing the annual wage withholdings instead of spending them in "pay as you go"(see above).

After a certain amount of juggling, the consequence would be 1) the elimination of copayments, bad debts from this source, and double insurances, 2) the elimination of "pay as you go" for wage withholdings, and 3) the establishment of a permanent terminal care reimbursement system, independent of Medicare but reimbursing it.. Future scientific advances might somewhat reduce the cost of terminal care, but in general medical scientific improvements in productivity

Medical costs of children neatly bifurcate for HSA use: rare catastrophic costs, and common small ones.

could all be applied to the health of younger people. As the system matures, the half-ing of cost for Medicare should become apparent to younger generations, but it will take time for the compound interest to build up to that level. At some point, the system should stabilize, and reverse funding for children could begin-- protected in the meantime by the fact that birth costs have already been absorbed for people who are currently alive.

Essentially all we have done is eliminate the secondary carrier and applied its revenue (plus a little massaging) to pay for terminal care. What happens to the premiums formerly paid on behalf of the secondary insurance? In all fairness, they should be added to the Medicare premium, because it is now carrying 100% of Medicare instead of only 80%. Everyone is better off, except the people who can't afford secondary insurance. Why not give them a tax deduction by allowing the Health Savings Account to pay their health insurance premium? After sixty years, they probably deserve that break.

Pearl #4 : Funding Newborns
and Children, a Special Case

We like to say newborns have a limitless horizon, and we also like to say their health costs are pretty cheap. Both things are true in a general way, but the occasional exceptions are quite often a financial disaster. An episode of extreme prematurity can cost a million dollars, and an extra chromosome can lead to a perhaps lovable life combined with the prospect of never becoming self-supporting, for the entire lifetime. The overall situation seems to demand a dual system: a catastrophic insurance for one group, and a highly predictable protection from the small, steady and universal health costs of the usual child. That seems simple enough, except the economic circumstances of the parents are an additional variable. And probably the unusual abundance of malpractice suits is another.

Let's dispose of the two side-issues hurriedly, in order to focus on the two types of health insurance required. It would be my position, the respectable members of the legal profession

Newborns have no money. Someone has to give them some.

have shirked their duty to clean up the profession's trial bar. The malpractice situation will not be rectified until they do. Secondly, most problems are the consequence of earlier solutions, so the changing environment is going to force us to modify the concept of "family plans" to pay for childbirth and children. That was once largely an accommodation to the need for the father's employer to find a way to pay the full health costs of his employee. Subsidizing large families was just part of the approach. But in effect it created a disincentive to hire employees likely to have large families, at a time when economists view economic growth as parallel to population growth. So the philanthropy of early company leaders eventually became a disincentive for later Human Resources departments, because it was now perceived as not in the company's interest to subsidize expensive employees. (It was probably the change from family businesses to stockholder corporations that was the main change.) That also applies to political squabbles about immigration, probably related to the tendency of immigrants to join one particular political party. Both of these mixed motives, malpractice and demographics, make the already overcomplicated health insurance problem, progressively more complicated.

Obstetrics is expensive for young parents, and with prematurity, malpractice costs, and genetic medicine in its future, finances may well get even more strained. The employer's contrivance of "family plans" will only serve as long as employers are willing to pay for it, and society seems to be moving away from even this option. Comparable provisions would apply to those who do not have employer-based insurance. A contrary but related incentive described later, is to add 20 or more years of compound interest at the beginning of the child's Health ("and Retirement") Savings Account. This extra extension of compound interest back to childbirth is about all little children would have to offer an insurance design, while everything else has some kind of drawback.

The goal we are therefore working toward might easily be called an exchange of the obstetrical and pediatric insurance costs to the baby's HRSA (Health and Retirement Savings Accounts, sort of in return for the protracted compounding. Even such remote return isn't a completely even exchange, but it's an exchange for something society is forced to give away, anyway. This is the exchange of income-generated funds for what had previously been a gift of someone else, usually the parents, sometimes the employer. It definitely is not a repayment of anything the baby paid for. Before that argument causes a flurry, let it be said that all obstetrical and pediatric costs already represent an unacknowledged gift to the penniless child from somebody. Whoever that is, could be called the true recipient of the gift. But since the money was generated by new investment, it benefits some people without hurting anyone else. Call it a gift if you please, but remember it lacks many of the features of what might otherwise be called a gift. Society gains an increase in the birth rate and probably the growth rate of the economy. It also gains some measure of relief from general disquiet arising from cost-shifting to a racial subgroup in straightened circumstances, who have traditionally responded to such pressures to the disadvantage of the educational system, and the choice of careers.

The direct purposes behind a shift are to add the extra years of compound interest to the baby's HSA, which effectively means adding it to everybody's HSA, a very sizeable sum, but perhaps a smaller one than more directly addressing what is causing so much trouble. The same people will generally pay the same amount in premiums, but a framework has even been created for shifting the social sands of the future in same-sex marriages and the like, just as well as penniless parents with expensive children. Every child would get catastrophic medical coverage, and routine childhood medical costs through two types of insurance. That is, every newborn would get an HRSA, and every newborn would have cost-free obstetrical and pediatric costs, which for the most part would be shifted from the parent's insurance arrangements. Since the catastrophes, obstetrical and pediatric, usually end up as a cost to society anyway, it is not extreme to investigate whether government subsidies may be appropriate for their insurance. In fact, it is not greatly different from the exchange Henry Kaiser invented, of making a gift to employees out of health insurance, which was already deductible from corporate taxes, and now is deductible from the employee's taxes. Since the unemployed and self-employed are excluded from that contrivance, this proposal -- in a sense, proposes we extend it to everyone.

The disincentive of the same premium for a family of three as a family of six, is obvious.

In somewhat greater detail, the proposal is to take the unsubsidized cost, give half to the mother's HSA, and the other half to the baby's HRSA, with the proviso that with both parent's consent they may assign it to the father's HSA, which makes up the other half of the cost. In essence, the rebate is split between parents unless one objects. (Hidden in the background is the suspicion that childbirth and death costs are both overtargeted for cost-shifting, just because they are unavoidable.). The ultimate source of the money is from the growth of the parent's HSAs from the birth of the child until the child's 25th birthday, a growth ratio for the money of about 6 to one. A single-premium health insurance for the child from birth to 25 might follow the same funding pattern. If you add the extra years to the other end, from age 70 to

90 however, the multiplier is 512 to one. Overall, the gift consists of a substantial subsidy for a substantial portion of the obstetrical and pediatric cost of having a child, but not a full subsidy and, one should hope, not coming from the taxpayer. The cost is reduced by the growth of HSA investments for a 25-year period, but ultimately is only reduced, not eliminated. There would be an initial cost to the parents, or in the case of poverty, a subsidy of about a fifth of the original cost. It would seem unwise to subsidize more heavily until we discover the response of the birthrate to this much subsidy, and the resulting public reaction. The subsequent ability of the parents then to modify the birthrate is an unexplored feature of this proposal, which could unfortunately extend into disputes about immigration policy.

Advantages. It's complicated to explain, fairly easy to understand. The advantage of an indirect solution lie in the establishment of a program which would considerably widen the appeal of an HRSA, extend its legitimacy to widen the period for compound interest to work, and make a start on a solution to a portion of healthcare which has previously defied complete resolution. It begins a program of a First and Last Year health insurance which by accordion principles would eventually replace the present disjointed one with another which matches the more probable scientific future. And all of this at relatively small cost, because of the multiplier effect of compound interest for twenty or thirty years.

Some time ago, it was originally imagined that Medicare could become overfunded, and result in surplus at the end. Grandparents could then transfer the excess to their children or grandchildren and pay for it all. Unfortunately, the finances of Medicare turned out to be so parlous, this approach must be more tentative; since it implies the money would still be there, ninety years later. It's going to take a long time to restore the trust in government we had a century ago; but on the other hand it took a century before that, to dispel the distrust of government with which we first crossed the Atlantic.

Being Born as a Pre-Existing Condition. Medical science is a wonderful thing, but it is impossible to imagine a lifetime without some medical costs, because everyone has the cost of the first year and the last year of life. The insurance problem is to define who must pay the bill. It seems unfair to assign all of the cost to the mother, but in today's world it is more visible the father may not always be available. The concept of family plan insurance was once stretched in order to include the employer-gifted concept, whether the mother worked for the employer or not. But the unfairness of charging the same premium for families of three, as for families of six was obvious, since it might later warp employment practices to include religious preferences. Everybody had a fairness argument, nobody had a workable plan.

Dispelling a Myth of the Past. It must be remembered, a "straightforward" funding proposal is not very simple, and for illustration an alternative is sketched out: Just have someone, the government in the case of indigents, contribute a hundred dollars to everybody's HSA at birth. Invest it in total market index funds for 90 years, and guarantee to pay a "big" lender back. The "big" lender finances the cost of the delivery and is repaid by the guarantee plus rebates from the two parties who benefit: the employer (or individuals who no longer have to pay the premiums for obstetrics), and the hospital which no longer sustains bad debts from this source. After appropriate payments from these indirect beneficiaries, the "baby's" HSA is the ultimate guarantor to the "big" donor. There should be some money left over, so the fund can be transferred to others and become perpetual in effect if not overtly. Unfortunately, this "straightforward" financing scheme is itself so complicated it will probably fail, and if not, its paperwork might eat up all its savings. In fact, the "big" lender might charge a higher interest rate than the HSA could earn. Let's see if a less straightforward approach works better.

Still Another First Twenty-Five Years of Life, Health Insurance Proposal. The first step is to get legal permission to do some unorthodox things. As a condition for providing the Last Four Years of Life benefit, which greatly favors Medicare recipients, the beneficiary agrees that somewhat less than ten thousand dollars may be transferred out of unused death benefits in Health Savings Accounts for the benefit of one child or grandchild, into the child or grandchild's HRSA. The ultimate source of this money is its growth following deposit, so it actually wasn't the depositor's money. Furthermore, with a birth rate of 2.1 per child-bearing woman, the math works out to one contribution per donor, no matter how many grandchildren there are, as long as the present birthrate remains constant. An insurance pool would be provided for childless situations. Because of higher interest rates at the end, payment may be delayed up to 21 years after death, just skirting the creation of perpetuities.

Upon the birth of the first child or grandchild, the money is transferred between HRSAs to the child's, meanwhile continuing to gather investment income for up to 21 years. It is paid out as a health insurance policy for half the cost of the birth of the child, plus the first 25 years of his life, and calculated to become exhausted at that time--except for the seed money to pay the next death benefit, which started to gather interest at birth. After age 25 the child is on his own. Age 25 is the moment of maximum career-choosing, but it is also the time of least financial responsibilities. It is the time to be taking risks, and therefore the time to be carrying least baggage.

Of course, health care might become the responsibility of the Affordable Care Act, the employer, or the individual, until the onset of Medicare. That issue remains to be seen. The rate of return on seed money is constantly monitored and re-adjusted to equal the final cash requirements, so the fund is gradually adjusted to be self-sustaining after the transition period. Our more realistic position is that age 25 is the point of lowest health risk in a lifetime, and it would not be shocking to leave the matter undetermined until the ACA issue gets more clarification. If by any chance the ACA is repealed or collapses, repairing the damage will probably occupy the full attention of Congress. It would then be particularly useful to have debated the various components of this plan in advance, searching for possible substitutes.

Features of First-Last Years Proposal. In the first place, interest on borrowed money is reduced or eliminated; that invisible cost disappears. Secondly, start-up costs can be postponed until financing accumulates, administration is in place, etc. Thirdly, the day would surely arrive sooner, when this system was self-financing, than with the reverse-mortgage approach. Although this system has a complicated start-up, it gets simpler and cheaper with time, and would be gradual. Ultimately, it might even solve a problem no one has solved -- unlocking childhood costs, the main obstacle to lifetime, or whole-life, health insurance -- at comparatively minor cost. That, too, would be a gradual phase-in, but it need not wait for a resolution of Affordable Care perplexities, using Health Savings Accounts in both cases as its foundation.

The Ultimate Outcome is the creation of a First and Last Years of Life Fund. The drain on Medicare, ACA, and regular health insurance is greatly reduced, along the way, but it may be unwise to aspire to eliminate these costs entirely; future generations can decide that. Meanwhile, the creation of a huge pool of ownership rights in the American economy should be addressed, with the first priority of reducing medical costs if possible. The creation of government control of the private sector should be vigorously avoided, as well as concentrating ownership control of corporations, by the accumulation of diffused stock voting control in millions of HRSAs. For this reason, the courts should recognize the unwisdom of permitting voting blocs, transfers of voting control, and other strategies to defeat the diffusion of control expressly intended.

Let's go back and look at the math. Money at 7% will double in value every 10 years, so if a newborn invests a dollar at 7%, it ought to be worth nine doublings in a lifetime, or 2,4,8,16,32,64, 128, 256, 512 increases -- that is, $512 in 90 years. Apparently it's rough and rounded off; a calculator on the Internet says it will be worth $515.69, based on two assumptions.

The first question is whether you will really get 7% on your HSA investment, and will it be compounded quarterly, following tradition for stock dividends to be issued every three months. Historically, that's fairly close, except the stock market averaged only half as much during recent market turmoils, suffering 30% dips in some years, 30% gains in others. In retrospect, it makes a whole lot of difference if you start investing just before a long recession, or just before the start of its recovery, so it may take 20 or 30 years to smooth out to the average. If you started investing at the age of 60, it's likely your results will mainly reflect your lucky birth year, even if you follow the precepts of "passive" investing in index funds of the entire stock market. A newborn risks a little. Approaching retirement, he may risk everything, but actual performance is unpredictable. Therefore, proposals to even it out in some way, are inevitable. But that should be the last step. Somehow, the public must learn to accept the fact that experimenters, risk-takers, are usually necessary as a first step in any major change.

Black Swans Another way of looking at this matter is to get out Yale Professor Roger Ibbotson's compendium of stock prices for the past century, and ignore the boilerplate reminder that past performance is no guide to future performance. Of course it is no guide, but it's all you have. Limiting your attention to the biggest 500 or 1000 corporations, which are a little safer, stock market total returns have risen fairly steadily at about 11% a year. However, inflation has eaten away at that by 3%, so the investor only realized 8% before the broker agent took out his own expenses. Moreover, the market is subject to 30% swings every few decades, and if you protect yourself from "black swans" by holding 40% in bonds, your returns average closer to 5%. "Active" investors try to run between the raindrops and do a little better, but the fees of an expert advisor absorb most of the profit, bringing you to about the same result. So unless you can somehow control the year of your birth, you are going to average somewhat less than 7%. The great challenge is to whittle away at these deductions. For example, this particular fund does not have a museum or a school to run, and thus has fewer ongoing cash needs to compete with depositor distributions. We must be careful not to add a burden in the name of prudence.

A newborn risks a little. Approaching retirement, he may risk everything.

But if you fool around with tips you heard at a party, you will almost certainly do worse. Taken all together, most conservative investors would say: an average investor is going to do worse than 7%, would be lucky to average 6%, and may well average about 5%. The challenge is to beat those numbers. According to our predictions, that won't be enough to pay for healthcare and retirement completely. But then, nothing will do it perfectly as long as we don't know where longevity will level out, or whether healthcare costs will fall, or what the economy will be like in the meantime. We must assign a more reasonable definition to a "decent" retirement, provide for a moderate one, and leave the differences to our own sources of wealth. It's essential to encourage that much financial Darwinism to keep one generation from attacking the income of another through other routes. But it's hard to see us going much further.

To doubt that investor distribution won't cover the entirety of health-care and retirement is definitely not trivial. It's worth trying however, in view of the gamble that science might do the rest, by curing some common diseases cheaply. And it's close enough to keep seeking that extra percent return, here and there. Since the existing financial system is so riddled with obvious inefficiencies, the chances of finding a breakthrough are not all that bad. The opportunities for people willing and able to take a risk are pretty attractive, but not everyone is temperamentally or financially wise to take them. Furthermore, everybody alive has already paid his birth costs somehow, so this childhood program can afford to be phased in last.

An average investor is going to do worse than 7%, would be lucky to average 6%, but may well average about 5%.

My guess is childhood funding will be greeted with reluctance. All the nasty talk about Wall Street makes a jarring clash with our soft and fuzzy notions about little kids. Kids run around in circles making excited noises, quite at variance with extensions of compound interest or contingency funds. But nevertheless, the math is close, and we cannot afford sentimentality. If we want to fund everybody's future, we need those years of extra compounding, and we need to face the fact that newborns will never have any money unless someone gives it to them. Those things won't change, and it helps nothing to drag out the discussion of it.

The system badly needs to put some money into itself, as early in life as possible, in the following areas:

Contingency Fund. Any person whose grandparent is willing to spend a thousand dollars at birth is very likely to win any healthcare bet. (It's likely to require much less than that, if we work hard at it.) There are lots of people who will never see a thousand dollars in one pile, in their whole lives. But there are millions of others who could easily afford it, and would become belligerent to be deprived of the liberty to do so. Is it really fair to prevent 80% of children from doing what 20% are unable to handle? Furthermore, a five year-old may seem impoverished at age five, and become a prosperous basketball star at twenty-five. With a swing of 500x from start to finish of a 90-year life expectancy, a contingency reserve eventually growing to a quarter or half-million dollars could easily be leveraged into a lifetime free of healthcare and retirement worries, and hence make a significant difference to lives. The issue of income disparities for newborns has little meaning until much later when the opportunity to exploit it has already eroded. There surely are many people who could afford this, and the leveraged effect on our economy might well unleash an unimaginable economic boom. Maybe it wouldn't, some would say; so a whole lot of people have lost a thousand dollars. So what? With enough income gain, these quarrels lose their significance. This contingency platform needs a demonstration program to make the gamble seem more realistic to its detractors.

The Last Four Years of Life Reinsurance. Medicare now costs about $12,000 per person per year, and the average person stays on Medicare for twenty years. Remember, average lifetime health costs are thought to be 300 or $350 thousand. But Medicare health costs themselves are also internally J-shaped -- a miniature version of full lifetime costs. Half of expenditures come in the last four years of someone's life. Let's simplify the slogan: Medicare is about half of healthcare cost, and the last four years are half of that. Advancing science may change this curve, which seems likely to reflect terminal illness. If it's approximately true, the transfer away of terminal care costs should reduce the cost of all healthcare by a quarter, and the cost of Medicare by half. The money isn't taken from anyone else and it isn' t created by magic. It takes advantage of the fact that terminal care comes at the end of longevity, which has grown to be almost ninety years. The rest is up to the stock market and the elimination of unnecessary costs. It it can't be done completely, it can be done in part. Its first step might be to eliminate the costs and profits of the secondary carrier, and add them to the compounding interest pool (see below). If the contingency fund pays for terminal care, it would come after a newborn expenditure of about a hundred dollars. That is to say, an expenditure of $100 (to the contingency fund at birth) could readily pay for cutting Medicare costs in half. If you know it is coming, why not save for it? The savings would express themselves as a reduction of deficit financing, payroll withholding, and Medicare premiums. These reductions could be gradual and in different priority, during the transition phase.

The first Twenty-five Years of Life Reinsurance. There is no way for newborns and children to pay for their own health costs; someone else has to shoulder this burden, usually the parents. Families of differing size are another complication, because small families resist paying for large ones. Because this problem has defeated conventional notions, we originally presented the possibility that grandparents should make the transfer, largely using investment gains to do it, but eventually for the relief of the parent generation. The parlous condition of Medicare makes this less certain. The first and last years of life would be largely funded by investment gains, and residual health costs would be much smaller and more equitably distributed. The precarious present system, of having the working third of the population support the non-working two thirds of the population, would be much reduced by a way shown to do it more safely.

Seemingly Shifting the Birth Costs to the Baby. Furthermore, it is important to emphasize that parents are currently paying the costs for children, so programs to fund childhood health would really mostly benefit their parents or their employer. Therefore, the most important part of this program is the re-arrangement of health costs between mother and child, which on first hearing seems to benefit the child. But it is unclear where the emancipation of women is going to take us. The perfectly understandable surcharge for women's health insurance, is nonetheless a factor in hiring patterns, and in family decisions about who is going to stay home as a caregiver. If the costs of health insurance for men and women were closer, it could help a lot. But they must not appear to violate the designs of Nature, or they will cause more trouble than they help. The two genders are in fact so different that attempts to even them out are often met with a contempt that is no help to the situation at all. A shift of health costs from the mother to the baby is a shift to someone else -- to a spouse or a consort who may well be isolated by his employer from the actual shift in costs. But it has a certain logic to it, and is about as far as you should dare to go. It also might help this problem to have a few states try it out as demonstration programs, because its effects may be unexpected.

Fun With Numbers. In summing up the reasons for a childhood insurance plan, one warning. These figures are derived from the published reports of CMS for 2015, probably reflecting 2014 data. Let's take the average Medicare benefits cost per capita as an example. To an East Coast resident, the figure of $12,000 per year per person seems a little low for terminal care. It is a national average, reflecting low rates for one state, high rates for another. Furthermore, a great deal of terminal care takes place at state expense in Medicaid. To enhance the recipients of ACA, such costs are shifted to Medicaid nursing homes. It's mainly Federal money, but it appears in the state ledgers and could quickly shift around, and end up as a Medicare expense. So the use of Last Years of Life cost-shifting might well shift the investment savings, but the net overall cost might also shift, or even seemingly rise, when new expenses are dropped on it. The transfer of terminal care to the contingency fund from Medicare would indeed save the consumer about $120,000, but the net Medicare cost could almost be made to seem what the political opponents want it to seem, even including an increase in Medicare expenditures as their last resort.

The Working Population, from age 25 to 65. Except for removing its destabilizing burdens, this proposal does not endeavor to change the Affordable Care Act. Although the author harbors opinions about it, this proposer has every intention of leaving the ACA to political, judicial, and electoral decision. For the practical purpose of avoiding discussion, the fiscal effects of the ACA are assumed to be neutral, in order to have as little effect on the broader discussion of program design as possible. In its present formulation, the ACA could disappear tomorrow, or it could last forever, and still make little difference to the essence of this proposal. But the chances the ACA budget rearrangements will be neutral, are apparently pretty slim.

SECTION THREE:

AN EARLY LOOK AT THE NECKLACE

The Two New Revenue Sources for HRSAs: Investments and Compound Interest

Two "new" revenue sources, which we need to discuss, are really quite old. But wide-spread use of third parties to pay medical bills diminished consumers' attention to their value. Patients become like Queen Victoria, indifferent to what it costs to run a household, even forgetting how to do it. We fit some details into the discussion of Health and Retirement Savings Accounts, but they are capsulized here for descriptive convenience, in an era when personal management has largely moved from junior high schools to the curriculum of graduate business schools. In the process, we have forgotten a timeless message: never let an agent manage your checkbook for you.

1. Compound Interest. Aristotle complained it gets more expensive to repay debts, the longer you take to pay them off. That's the debtor's viewpoint, of course. The creditor's view of it is, the longer the better. But restated as a neutral mathematical comment, an essential feature of compound interest is that both principal and effective interest, rise over time. To repeat: income rates (and/or borrowing costs) from a debt, increase with duration. About half the capital of every major corporation consists of debt, so even owning common stock has some of the quality of being a debtor. Furthermore, this effect is seen sooner, with quite small rises in nominal interest rates. A graph of sample interest rates demonstrates this simple truth with greater clarity:

As a result of centuries of haggling and experimentation, most modern loans charge interest rates of 5-15%. That's an enormous swing, but only for long-term investing. It makes little difference whether this range of rates reflects the supply of money in the economy, or the vigor of the economy, or something else macroeconomic. So long as rates remain steady, or even if they are changing at a slow steady rate, borrowers and lenders can reach agreement and negotiate a long-term loan. If there is uncertainty about rates in general, they may rise precipitously, so all borrowers know to keep loans as short as possible, and creditors quickly raise rates when they must cover longer time periods.

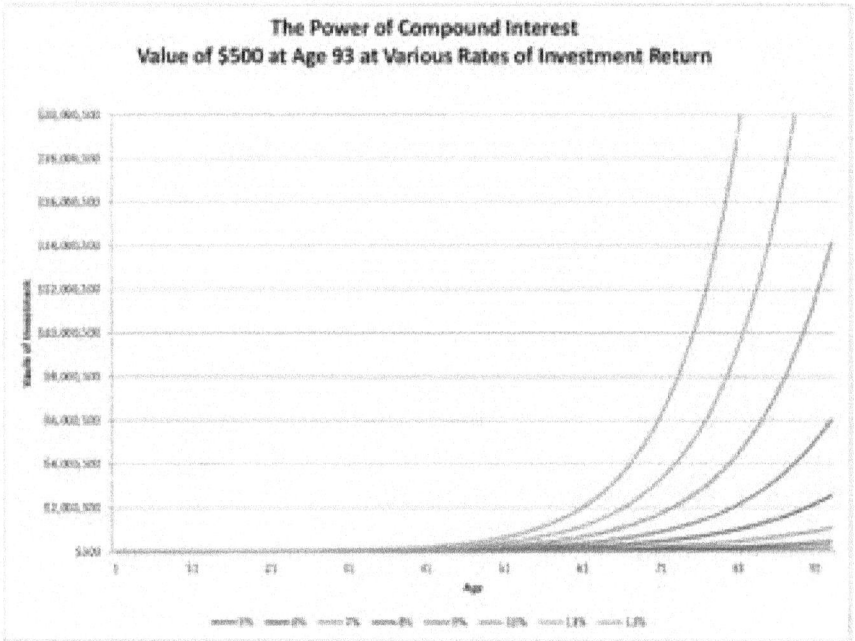

The Power of Compound Interest
Value of $500 at Age 93 at Various Rates of Investment Return

The moral is, as you become older you tend to become a creditor, so adjust your mentality from borrowing short to lending long. For centuries, nobody thought much about this invisible equilibrium, because life expectancy was stable at the Biblical threescore and ten -- and in fact only twoscore. But suddenly around 1900, life expectancy at birth began to rise, and starting in 1950 it entered a steep climb from forty-seven to eighty-four years. Thirty-year loans remained the extreme, however, because the proportion of those who would chisel you doesn't seem to change much. Stagecoach robberies went away, but inflation took their place. Underneath it all, governments prefer to expand the currency supply rather than raise interest rates, printing repayments rather than repaying them. Interest rates are, as they say, volatile. Within limits, they are also malleable.

Nevertheless, the expansion of longevity created a new opportunity. Long-term investment was more profitable for everybody. The upturn in interest rates was relatively negligible for the first forty years of compound interest, but progressively quite handsome after that. In practical terms, buy-and-hold became the better strategy. The difference of a tenth of a percent means little in a ten-year loan, but it can create a stupendous profit in a ninety-year loan. One suspects the interest rate on a bank loan has more to do with the debtor's working life (the period available for confident repayment) than his life on earth. In this book we concentrate on the creditor, whose lifespan should not affect interest rates as much as it affects his opportunity to enjoy money, so long as he has some of it. But a long life without money at the end of it is a fearsome prospect, indeed.

2. Equity Index Investing. The stock of only one company (General Electric) was a member of the Dow-Jones Industrial Average a century ago. By definition, the DJII always contains thirty leading stocks; others have been replaced many times. It takes a long time to become a household name, and by the time an investor has heard the name, it is often ready to decline. Active investing, meaning sell one to buy another, was once quite necessary for success. Unless fading leaders are replaced by new leaders however, the average would fall behind, But it is easy to see the average has moved steadily upward, so it must be actively managed by someone.

If you are careful to avoid the spongers and the fly-by-nights, the investment world is rapidly changing, mostly for the better. To some extent this reflects a flight from the bond market which governments deal with, but most investors now think total market index funds are safer. When the Federal Reserve forces banks to buy its bonds through "Quantitative Easing", the supply of bonds goes up and so the price goes down. "Passive" investing is certainly easier for the small investor to deal with, and investors are responding.

Later we will try to take advantage of one obvious flaw in such investing. If a single investment represents thousands of companies, investor control is diluted to meaninglessness. The only effective control over management then resides in the shares which are not held by funds; and even there, more and more corporate control rests with insiders and managers. The effect of such a trend is not merely that manager salaries are inflated, but the corporation becomes less responsive to the consumer public. Its legitimate business plan is to make a profit, but to make a short-term profit at the expense of long-term profits is not so defensible. Because of the corporate shield, many corporations borrow too much, risk too much, and collapse too often, but their managers often walk away with riches. If Health and Retirement Savings Accounts really get popular (at last count, they only had thirty billion dollars invested), its counterweight of stock ownership should help restrain consumer prices. Nevertheless, experience seems to show that competition between companies has been a more effective guardian of public interest, than stockholder control of individual competitors.

HSAs collect money when it is not needed, spend it decades later when it is badly needed, and invest the money during the interval, tax-free. The longer the interval, the more it earns. And with careful application of the principles of compound interest and index investing, the earnings are considerably magnified. If your Christmas Savings Fund earns more money, it reduces the effective cost of what you buy. But if you are careless, investment fees and inflation will ruin everything. So that, in sum, is another message.

Diagnosis Based Payment: A Warning

I was sitting in the Congressional hearing room when it happened. A proposal from the hospital association was made to Congress in 1983 that instead of paying hospitals for each step of treatment, they should be paid by the diagnosis, and Congress soon agreed to the idea for Medicare. This system was to be limited to helpless inpatients. The idea had some good features: if a patient had to be fed with a spoon, he had little interest in the cost of his treatments. Under these circumstances, market mechanisms would never restrain the cost of hospitalized patients. If they were anaesthetized, it was even more true.

The problem was to put a price on thousands, even millions, of diagnoses with enough difference in cost to warrant a code number. The fifty year-old coding system of the AMA called *Standard Nomenclature of Diseases and Operations*, had room for a hundred million diagnosis codes, of which perhaps two million were in use.

DRG: An Object Lesson for Control Freaks With Little Interest in What They Are Controlling.

It was a useful classification in the days when hospitals and Natural Science museums were much alike, cataloging and classifying different objects. But record librarians were in a position to see what their main activity was really like. It was gathering the various pieces of previous admissions in order to be useful in managing a new episode for an individual. For this, a new code was less work for the record librarians: the *International Classification of Diseases*, which reduced the number of diagnoses in practical use to about a thousand. When greater detail was needed, it was simpler just to look it up, and record librarians knew very few doctors except pathologists actually did that. So hospitals were ordered by accrediting bodies to use ICD coding, and save administrative costs. After Congress made its payment decision, a committee was formed to cut the thousand down to two hundred with similar payments, and lo, the DRG (*Diagnosis-Related Groups*) were created. All hospital inpatients were assigned one of two hundred codes, within which the size of the payment was a dominant sorting feature. Before long, in-patients were accordingly charged one of two hundred prices. The pathologists objected, and produced their own modernized coding system, *SNOMed*. Forget it, it was too much work, cost too much, it was too hard. (By the way, the number of DRG codes is already back up to a thousand.)

So in this way, by arranging the assignment of costs to codes, Medicare and the hospital coding clerks took over the job of pricing. No doctor understood what in the world they were doing. And by steps familiar to accountants, the DRG was enlarged back to a thousand codes and internally arranged to come out paying the hospital a 2% profit margin for inpatients. Since we were running a 3% inflation at the time, the effective push was on-- to move in-patients to the out-patient area. No matter how many tests, no matter how long the patient stayed, the DRG came out to produce a 2% profit margin. The cost the insurance had to pay was lessened, the costs the hospital actually incurred, became the hospital's problem. Meanwhile, interest rates were low, so new outpatient buildings seemed cheap. Pretty soon, hospitals were paying doctors above-market prices to fill the outpatient area. There's more to say, but the idea is clear. Once you find a rationing tool, the accountants are in charge, the doctors are out, and eventually would be really out. And the beauty part of it was, no one understood what was happening, or who did it. Except you will find a lot of empty out-patient buildings when the music stops.

Electronic Medical Records

The electronic medical record had a great flurry of excitement about 1980, and I was one of its earliest proponents. I wrote my own program in the Basic language to produce bills and insurance claims forms, and to serve as the basis for adding diagnoses, lab work and prescriptions. It took about a year of my spare time, worked very well in my office, and is available for anyone who wants it. It had two flaws, and it still has two flaws. After a fruitless effort to simplify physician input, I abandoned that particular effort as taking too much of my time.

That's still the case, thirty years later. Programmers have a habit of telling the boss something can't be done when it is merely inconvenient to do it, and doctors absolutely will not tolerate doing something some lesser-paid person can do for them. Some variant of the Google search engine might suffice for coping with physician input, particularly if combined with Dragonfly voice recognition. Eventually, someone will conquer this beast, but it turns out to be harder than it looks, and nerdy doctors have turned their attention from data entry to Big Data. Meanwhile, programmers have avoided the task of simplifying something which could be simplified, just because it requires acknowledging that somebody else's time is worth more than their own. The time for excitement about data entry has passed, while the problem remains incompletely solved. If you were going to win a Nobel prize, it wasn't going to be for data entry perfection.

The second physician obstacle is that computers generate far more information than anyone has time to read. The white blood count is vital when appendicitis is being considered, but it just bulks up the chart thirty years later. So what is needed is an automatic summarization system, with hooks back to the original data in the rare instance where retrieval is needed. Since medical care is constantly changing, the summarization algorithm must change with it. It's a big job, and somehow billions of dollars have been expended trying to do something else the doctor never asked for. The new danger is that some malpractice lawyer will discover a point vital to his case has been omitted from the summarization (but not the bulk record) without the doctor's knowledge, even though it seems no longer vital to treatment of the patient in the future. For a long time, I merely smiled when people told me the EMR was more trouble than it was worth. But recently I have read of the astounding amounts of money (thirty billion dollars have been mentioned) which have been devoted to this mess, much of which is pretty cute but nobody asked for it. Apparently, the doctors who advised the program let the big-shot millennials who actually wrote the code do the real directing, because it seemed worthwhile to spend billions to accomplish their personal goal of payment by diagnosis instead of by procedure. Maybe that's how you subdue a bucking broncho, but the doctors work around you until you seem to be winning. And then they quit.

If someone had the bad judgment to put me in charge of this circus, I would immediately limit the archiving to data which can be automatically generated, and rest content with reports of lab and x-ray reports from this source. And then I would advertise for someone to produce workable physician data entry, as well as generate periodic automatic summarization. Until these two features pass approval by seasoned physicians, we would just have to get along with paper records. This is essentially what I told some meetings of 1980 enthusiasts. But it hasn't happened, yet, so the system progressively antagonizes a group they cannot command and cannot do without. Herding cats, I believe it is called.

The Place of Interest Rates in All This

We regularly used 7% interest rates in this discussion for the convenience of doing math in your head. Periodically, we warn the average investor probably won't achieve 7% consistently, although average results are not far from it. We are not on any gold or other monetary standard, where in the past the prevailing interest rate could emerge from the ratio of gold supply to population as a surrogate for the current economy. It must be mentioned however, that America holds seven or eight thousand tons of gold in Fort Knox, as a sort of unofficial gold standard in reserve. Officially, our Federal Reserve adjusts the money supply to a 3% annual growth target, which is an expedient which works most of the time. Right now is not one of those times, and the Fed is plainly unable to achieve a stated 2% inflation target. The reason for this is not entirely clear, although many suspect we have issued so much debt the interest-rate "price" was depressed. So it is somewhat unclear what our normal interest rate should be, or even when rates will level off. All of our assumptions of 7% must eventually be adjusted to the real rate, but we aren't entirely clear what that should be. Like the Federal Reserve, we must operate on the assumption that present relative values will persist in the economy. They may not.

The upheavals of Greece, Brexit, and the 2016 Presidential elections are a hint others see this untethered interest rate as an opportunity to change it to their advantage. Generally, debtors favor lower interest rates, and all governments are debtors. Conservatives generally adopt the posture that absolute rates do not matter, what matters is to maintain stable interest rates for the present duration of your main assets. However, this pressures a shortening of the duration of loans, which have gone from a formerly typical thirty years to ten. Carried too far, this makes capitalism impossible, and picks up supporters who favor that inclination.

Based on these two paragraphs, we favor the purchase of common stock in some form, over debt in some form, as an investment for Health Savings and Retirement Funds. The bond market is so much larger than the stock market, this situation probably will not change much. Even if the economy is destroyed, and the stock market will then be destroyed, stocks are likely to be destroyed last. Cowboys and bandits may dabble in derivatives or active investing, but the ordinary investor is urged to consider total market index funds without high fees as their safest long-term haven. Buy and hold, but don't buy and forget. Two or four times in a lifetime, you may have to be prepared to do something else.

Bewildering Prices for Medical Care

Newsmedia speak of medical "prices", the government speaks of medical "cost" -- what's the difference? Well, for fifteen years in my practice, and before that for thousands of years, prices and costs were nearly the same thing, or at least bore some relation to each other. The person who did the work set the price, and the person who paid the bill agreed to the price.

But out on the West coast they told us Henry J. Kaiser during World War II had expanded the idea of the Mayo Clinic into a pre-paid health system of clinics and pre-agreed patients, paying a set annual fee for all the care you could use in a year. By 1970 I was sent by my local medical society to see what this was all about. I learned a lot, including the main thing which made it so cheap rested on two government tax exemptions, one for the employer and a second one for the employee. They recruited doctors with the promise of relieving them of the business nuisances of medicine, plus instant practice-builders of employee groups of patients. Doctors in the neighborhood didn't like Kaiser at all, particularly after the *Maricopa* decision of the U.S. Supreme court made it an antitrust violation for doctors to do the same thing. For lawyers reading this, it is a particular irritant that this decision was 4-3 (not a majority), based without a trial of the facts, solely on upholding a motion of summary judgment.

Turning from historical legalities to practical economics, turning that is, from one doctor both doing the work and setting the price, into a third party with no doctors setting the price, the third party (the insurance company) paid its own reimbursement price. So not only did the physicians eventually lose control of pricing their own work, but that price rapidly drifted away from the audited cost in a capricious manner, responding to forces entirely unrelated to medical care. The accountants protested this lack of relationship between cost and price, and it was a legal requirement for hospitals to report (but not make public) the ratio of prices to cost. While the ratio was always high, it was also extremely variable. In effect, a fact demonstrated when the "diagnosis-related" system fixed inpatient costs by groups rather than individually, the disparity was only used to compete for out-patients with outside market prices. However, instead of forcing hospital prices down, it enticed drug companies to force prices up, often to absurd levels. Some hospitals negotiated discounts and applied them as invisible mark-ups to the uninsured patients. Cheap mortgages stimulated hospital building, and the situation spiraled out of control, as it does in any inflation. Nobody ever cured an inflation, except with brute force and lots of pain.

In our system, the money supply is governed by the Federal Reserve issuing and/or buying bonds. In so doing, it is issuing unheard-of amounts of debt for which there is no market, forcing interest rates down. Although the Japanese allow their central bank to buy common stock, Congress is adamant that buying ownership of corporations amounts to Communism with a demonstrated history of universal failure. Congress will probably never permit government take-over of corporation ownership, but Mr. Obama simply spent money beyond Congressional limitation and dared Congress not to pay the bill (and thus to ruin our national credit). Congress is not compelled to make a rational choice between inflation and government control of the private sector, but you can be certain it has been discussed.

I never took a course in economics but it seems to me, a couple of million individual citizens building up half-million dollar portfolios of indexed common stock might provide an adequate balance for three trillion dollars of excess debt. That is, holders of Health Savings Accounts would hold voting control of corporations, without the organization to abuse that power, and that power could never pass into foreign hands because it is contingent on American-based health care. Plenty of other regulations, good and bad, would have to be added for the system to become stable and tamper-proof, but it's a suggestion for debate and study of a possible solution to an entirely unrelated subject. One for which there has been an international shortage of fresh suggestions.

The Central Argument of Our Times:
Balancing Prices Between Costs and Revenue

Somehow, it seems necessary to reiterate the very simple model of the marketplace: the housewife with a basket, bargaining with a farmer at the back of his wagon. The price is set by supply and demand: she has to get home to cook dinner, he has to get home to his farm. As the vegetables in the back of the wagon dwindle, she has to pay more to get something. When it gets later and his wagon is still full, he has to lower his price.

But the Industrial Revolution changed the balance: as mass production grew, more people were hired, including an accountant to keep track of what it cost to make something. The factory couldn't sell below average cost, else it went out of business. Price was still set by supply and demand, so if there was a margin of profit, there could be disputes about how to divide it. If the factory got big enough, some of the workers inevitably had no idea what their contribution was worth. That became increasingly true on both sides of the equation, both for the buyer and the seller. The use of a Health Savings Account at least re-simplifies the price matter for the buyer, who has to authorize each transaction. Ultimately, he says yes he will pay the medical price, or no he won't. Only when he is too sick to care, should the insurance take over the bargaining. Unfortunately, he has no idea whatever about the audited costs of the other party in the transaction, so he has to rely on supply-and-demand to make the price seem right and fair.

In a typical hospital of three or four thousand employees, or a typical drug company with fifty thousand of them, the typical employee may have no idea of the fairness of the top boss, the CEO, or his lieutenants getting big salaries. The employees and stockholders might be underpaid, or the customers overcharged. There was plenty of proof that both injustices could occur, but no proof whether in general, the public was charged fairly for a vitally necessary product. Enter insurance and government control, to fill that gap.

Insurance prices are set by insurance competition, so the anti-trust statutes at least try to be satisfied insurance was not a monopoly. Healthcare is one step removed, and not very transportable. So health anti-trust is a somewhat more local thing, although consumer groups tend to look for foreign comparisons. Governments are a slightly different matter; they can be as unfair as they please as long as they get re-elected. But in a sense, King George III of England and Benjamin Franklin together, long ago discovered the real resistance to that idea. When London's St. Paul's Cathedral was struck by lightning, Ben Franklin (then living a few blocks down the street) was quite reasonably called to consult. He said the church needed a needle-shaped lightning rod. But King George wanted a copper ball, and he was King. In time, King George got his copper ball, but lost much of his kingdom for his royal heedlessness of facts. In the long run, Franklin won the argument, but lost his British loyalty. Apparently, he said words to the effect, "Who the hell do you think you are, telling me about lightning rods?" Historians will differ about which of them was being more unwise.

Fundamentally, the issue in pricing seems to be the currency. No one denies the government must control the currency, and very few want to see a return to the gold standard. Getting more specific, it seems reasonable to allow the the government to water the currency in order to preserve the nation's health -- during some sort of national disaster. But it is totally unreasonable to watch the currency get watered in order to balance the Federal budget without raising taxes, or some other contrived excuse to lower interest rates. The suggestion of funding healthcare with huge internal reserves may not seem pertinent to this imbalance, but it is.

The very idea of a few elected officials making such a decision without public support, calls into question the wisdom of using the power of the public purse to serve as a fail-safe mechanism for overspending on healthcare. If a hundred million voters stake their future healthcare on a stable currency (in the HSA way), it would not prohibit government from acting as re-insurer of last resort. But it would make it a whole lot harder to water the currency, in the name of better healthcare.

Limits on What Can be Promised:
Healthcare Plus a Modest Retirement.

This study of Health Savings (and Retirement) Accounts was begun thirty years ago, and with increased intensity in the past five years. During most of that time, paying for health costs was the central concern. Paying a big chunk of health costs would be an achievement, paying for it all would be an impossible dream. Therefore, paying for the whole healthcare system became a goal of my proposals -- to extend the duration of the compound interest generated. If it fell short, well, it paid for a big part of it. Either way, we could afford to leave Medicare alone. But once Medicare came into focus as the main impediment to solving an even bigger problem for exactly the same age group, "saving" it becomes a relatively smaller issue. There had to be some money left over for retirement living, which meant all of Medicare must first be covered, and then, new revenue must be found. The quality of care must not be injured, and -- most of all -- public opinion must be re-directed. This is a specialist's game, but the public is now the supervising coach. Whether they realize it or not, a dependable agent is what they are going to need. And agency has a long history of imperfection.

Resource Assessment. Adding up all the other economies of Health (and Retirement) Savings Accounts, but now also including the retirement costs, the most optimistic goal is that *HRSAs might pay for substantial health costs, and some but not all retirement costs.* Any politician who promises more is counting on a research miracle curing one or more expensive diseases. And the warning is: you will probably get less. Much of the shortfall comes from difficulty stating a "decent" retirement payment which would satisfy most people. What's enough for a Trappist monk is not enough for a movie star, and what will be called decent in 60 years is pretty hard to say. So the most we should promise is: **healthcare**

The New Goal: Legitimate Healthcare, plus a modest retirement.

plus some retirement; supplement more generous retirement as you are able. Even promising that much is a stretch, but is certainly superior to healthcare plans without the discipline of individual ownership. Unfortunately, it forces the individual to some choices he must make for himself, versus allowing some big anonymous corporation to do it all for him at a hefty markup. Let's specify the two big dangers he must navigate:

Imperfect Agents Theoretically, the best result anyone could provide would be to give a newborn baby a couple hundred dollars at birth, let a big corporation do the investing, and pay a million dollars worth of bills over the next ninety years on his behalf, at no charge. The long investing period would provide some astonishing returns, and it would be entirely carefree for the customer. But that really overstates things quite a lot.

Unfortunately experience over thousands of years has demonstrated agents eventually extract much of the profit for themselves. When they form large organizations with a business plan to maximize profits, the plan becomes institutionalized. Countless kings have been known to shave the edges of gold coins, even more have been found to have employed inflation of the currency to pay their own bills. Investment managers are almost invariably well compensated, usually for mediocre returns to the investor. William Penn, the largest private landholder in history, was put in debtors prison by his wayward agent, as was Robert Morris, the financier of the American Revolution. Whole-life insurance companies are the closest approximation to an agent for a Health Savings Account who might propose to get paid a level premium for decades before paying out a limited benefit for a dead client. They seem to survive by promising a single defined fixed-dollar benefit, and counting on inflation to work for them as it does for dictators, overseen by a politically appointed insurance commissioner. Unfortunately, they have the moral hazard of falling back on other surviving competitors to bail out a bankruptcy, and the political hazard of trying to force premiums downward for the taxpayer without any reliable benchmark. Just how much they have been rescued by lengthened longevity is something only an actuary knows. Long ago, the situation was summarized by the question, "And where are the customers' yachts?"

Inexperienced Solo Management. If Warren Buffett had an HSA, he would have no problem managing it, and neither would a great many other savvy folks. The problem is to make the management so simple and standard that expenses can be kept low without injuring investment returns, for the average citizen. This consideration almost drives the conclusion that lifetimes would be best divided into at least three component parts, with benchmarks and averages published more regularly, since the medical and beneficiary problems divide into the same three (childhood, working age, and retirement) components. It begins to look as though a new profession of fee-for-service advisors needs to become educated and distribute themselves widely, perhaps in local bank branches, and they must develop a professional ethic of fiduciaries. As will be described in later sections, the need is for the income stream at least to be kept in balance with the probable expenditures, adjusted for inflation or deflation -- and volatility. It is not to achieve the maximum possible revenue return, regardless of risk. That is to say, the purpose of the HRSA is not to make as much money as possible, but to be sure as much medical need as possible can be provided by the revenue available. Let's put it all in a nutshell: There's a big difference between designing a system to cover a public need inexpensively -- and designing a business model to make a profit. But that's not nearly as big a problem, as doing both at the same time, because it tempts the agent to be too timid.

After Assessing Obstacles Comes Strategy. Most HSAs make cash payments with a debit card compatible with long-term passive investing (utilizing total market index funds) by staying within the stream of cash deposits, on behalf of inexperienced investors and for otherwise unevaluated accounts. If deposits fall, or expenses are unexpected, they may need reserves. Theoretically, a single investor with a single advisor may reduce this need and improve the overall return. However, there's a technical problem: the earning period is not the first stage of life; it's the second, following nearly a third of life in childhood and educational dependency or debt. Health expenses in the childhood third of lifespan may be comparatively small, but the earning capacity of children is

If you spend too much too early, you won't have anything left for later.

essentially zero. This unconquerable fact leads to splitting investment considerations into three stages, the first and last thirds subsidized by the middle one. The result is, two systems feeding off the middle third in opposite ways, requiring opposite approaches. Somehow, it must all come out in balance at the end. And remember, it starts with a deficit in the obstetrical delivery room unless we re-arrange something else. That's the biological situation, against which financial systems must lean their weight. Therefore, there is a need for different agents for different age groups. This has not yet been fully worked out, so there is a constant need for transferability of accounts between agents.

Dubious Wisdom: Adding Incentives to Health Savings Accounts on Behalf of Other Linked Accounts

Government programs tend to have a "one size fits all" quality, growing in part from the Constitutional requirement for equal justice under the law. Most of them make no mention of what to do with left-over funds, usually implying they return excesses to the pool for recycling. Supposedly that reduces the cost for everyone else. Sometimes, of course, it raises employee salaries, buys battleships, or is otherwise spent for things we didn't specify. A much better default rule would be to return unspecified excesses to the original contributor, as an incentive to keep his spending lean and mean. But that's someone else's Crusade; we just urge it to be examined each time the matter arises.

Cookie-cutter similarity is exaggerated by the way legislation is created. Each Congressman represents nearly a million constituents, far too many to be running for re-election every two years with scant time left to legislate. The laws are consequently too general, are revisited too infrequently, and leave too much to the Judicial branch and the administrative agencies to settle. Congress increasingly resembles a Board of Directors, rather than the source of legislation, ultimately lacking the power to control the President by picking him. For this reason, we hear the British parliamentary system praised, since the Prime Minister is chosen by the ruling party. My own feeling is Congressmen are not able to devote enough time to the job of legislating mainly because they spend so much time in the telephone call center, soliciting election funds within the hearing of their leadership. The deluge of business is ultimately the balance point of leverage in the system. Let's examine some issues which are not urgent, but eventually must be settled by these harried law-makers.

We have stumbled onto the clear linkage between paying for healthcare, and subsequently being forced to pay for the resulting extended retirement, which is an unexpected but inevitable consequence of improving health care. Although the cost of healthcare has been a national concern, extended longevity proves to be potentially even more expensive, expressed as a lump sum at age 65. That's because a completed retirement fund becomes a constantly shrinking asset once you retire, whereas Medicare is only spent when you get sick. Furthermore, retirement will soon last a third of a lifetime (or more), so it is awkward to suggest a defined price for it. Everyone, even someone who is quite rich, is afraid to spend retirement funds for fear of running out of money during a particularly expensive terminal episode, like some of the cancer treatments now making an appearance. Homogeneous nations like the Scandinavians seem willing to carry equal retirement to a national level, for approximately the same reason socialism is more popular there. A homogeneous people are more willing to trust each other to "re-insure" the whole population in unpredictable circumstances. But our society seems headed in the opposite direction of diversity. These are not parallel goals.

Socialism is mainly unpopular in America if carried beyond issues of mere subsistence, because of its tendency to reduce work incentives. So it's a circular argument usually growing out of famines and genocides. For example, raising the retirement age might ease financial strains, but instead many people just want to quit work at age fifty, while others see no reason to retire at all. Unfortunately, workaholics resent the suggestion their extra income should support others who prefer to quit work. The difficulty is magnified by first supporting thirty million people who are plainly unable to work, plus at least an equal number who hate the kind of work they do. The outcome is a diverse nation seemingly resistant to government protections which guarantee more than bare survival, in constant contention with a subpopulation which yearns for education during the first third of their lives, and another subpopulation which yearns for expensive leisure during the last third of their lives.

If that's a fair analysis, there will always be divergence in luxury for retirements, and therefore a constant propaganda war between fairness to the poor and fairness to their more visibly successful competitors. The term "Social Darwinism" captures that flavor. At least for a long time to come, the amount available for individual pensions at retirement age will be a scorecard for a successful life. Both public boasting and envious criticism should therefore be discouraged, but the lifelong incentive to be frugal cannot be ignored. If we can manage this paradox, the incentive can be used as a silent reminder that what you frittered away as a youth, might have been used to improve your retirement. At the very least, the public might be reminded government debt lowers long-term interest rates, intentionally lowered in order to stimulate short-term growth of the economy. But to paraphrase John Keynes, "In the long run, we are all retired." Eventually, we must all live on what we saved, and debts we agreed to must be repaid. What we now seem to have, are incentives to retire early, and incentives for the government to inflate away the cost by suppressing interest rates.

Therefore, if unifying the finances of medical care and retirement at any age, is an incentive to be medically frugal, why not unify the incentives for all things medical? Otherwise, the landmark moment becomes the termination of your present means of support, the termination of your present mortgage, or graduation from your present school. There is general agreement, medical costs have risen so fast because there is nothing else to spend *earmarked* medical money on, except frivolous medical care. As we said earlier in the book, there is reason to suppose the success of Health Savings Accounts lies in the powerful incentive provided by retirement needs, offered as a use for left-overs from healthcare. The roll-over of an HSA into an IRA provides an alternative, and the tax deduction for health of an HSA provides a preferred, but not mandatory, outlet.

If, one by one, other funding sources for healthcare flow into an HSA, healthcare at all ages is provided with a unified incentive to be frugal. Health insurance of one form or another may resist the HSA alternative, but if we are correct, the market will force it. Because medical care seems destined to concentrate among elderly people, it seems urgent to provide this incentive to Medicare first. Of all

One logical place to begin, is to pay a bounty into an HRSA for subnormal spending during the previous year places, Medicare is the least desirable place to be employing deficit financing, pay-as-you-go financing, or other mechanisms to make it appear to be less expensive than it is. Medicare is where serious expensive disease concentrates, and that trend continues. Because of stretched finances, one logical place to begin, is to pay a bounty into an HSA for subnormal spending during the previous year. The compound-interest beauty of this approach is: the younger you do it, the more it will help; and so that idea might be built into it,too.

Flexibility is also an incentive for almost any program. We have mentioned several ways to enhance Medicare's revenue and there seems no reason to limit the choices. The transition from Medicare as we know it is likely to be a long one, and family circumstances may change several times during the phase-in. If the individual could contribute to the contingency fund, or to the Last Year of Life fund, make choices for increased benefits for late retirement --and flexibility for anything else anyone can suggest, the bookkeeping may become more complicated, but the attractiveness of Medicare improves.

Attention might be paid to the individual's ability to apportion the distribution of his nest-egg at the time of retirement, until the time later on when he writes his last will and testament. There will be an irresistible tendency to overestimate personal retirement needs, in order to avoid exhausting them too soon, and that should be relied upon. On the other hand, these requirements are often abruptly changed by illness, or death of a spouse. There might be several contingency funds, with different rules for invading them. These warnings are issued in full realization most people cannot see so far ahead, and most people will be a long way from achieving their own goals.

With such general ruminations in mind, it seems inadvisable to limit choices without good cause, or provide for handling exceptional cases with some sort of required approval. Doing otherwise might lead to forcing some people to reject a job opportunity, or else to buy insurance they do not need. Or to encourage inflation to minimize the unfairness to a surviving spouse, to force reduction of his/her lifestyle. For the first few decades at least, constraining the choices at certain critical points should operate on a sort of common-law or Court of Equity process. As the issues gradually surface, they are slowly resolved. The country grows increasingly restless about the intervention of administrative agencies without adequate oversight by the court system, at the same time it distrusts the courts. The problem is not so much incompetent courts, as the design of a system dumping decisions on them which might better be made by the individuals. Once more, the problem of too little congressional time surfaces. At present, the tendency to flexibility is to reduce it, and most of the public prefers otherwise.

Marriage Laws. Broken marriages, whether broken by death or design, are too common to justify immobilizing their future direction. A lawyer dominated legislature must recognize the danger of too much power in the hands of the trial bar when dealing with life-long savings of either party to a divorce, or both, or prior expenditures of the couple for health purposes. Or unanticipated contingencies which occur after the separation of a couple. It will be a long time before we have settled what is best to do about serial marriages of homosexuals, or marriages of intersex couples, or no marriages at all. The courts dealing with lifetime health and retirement funds should at least have a defined outlet for the special insights their role provides, because the country will need to hear those insights.

Special Treatment of the Handicapped. Not only do handicapped people of all varieties have increased healthcare expenses, they have special laws dealing with their problems. These may conflict with what is generally best to do about lifetime health and retirement funds. It is unwise to freeze the rules before the exceptions become evident. Retirement is now commonly thirty years long; relationships can change. Freed of obligations to minor children, they may even change more rapidly.

Expatriate Citizens and Conflicts Between States. It is comparatively common for citizens who were foreign-born, to retire to the nation of their birth because it is cheaper to live there. They become subject to devaluations of the foreign currency, and prey to agents who purport to help them, just as residents of different state jurisdictions become subject to conflicting mandates. If the host country abuses them, they present a problem for the State Department.

The list of potential conflicts with flexibility is very long, and these are only examples of it. The basic point is that a mechanism should be created to deal with long term exceptions to laws which envisioned a much shorter horizon and many fewer linkages.

A Small Gamble for Big Returns

Although the Pearls on a String design seems to hold great promise for matching American health finances to the medical lifetime it proposes to finance, it contains the flaw of taking 90 years to test it in action from birth to death. That is, almost no one would live long enough to know if it, for certain, worked the way it promised. But on the other hand, there is a significant chance scientists will discover cures for many expensive diseases during the next ninety years-- and so it might work far better than anyone expected. What kind of bet would we be asking people to take?

To be blunt about it, if some fool blows up the earth with atom bombs, it scarcely matters what kind of health insurance anybody had. And if some expensive diseases are cured, all you get for your hundred dollars is a return of $5000 to $29,000. So the main risk is mismanagement. A good idea badly managed can be as risky as a poor idea. Mismanagement includes poor design at the beginning, or poor management along the way. In this case, it's pretty much up to Congress, to neglect it or to use it as a piggy bank. So it's a little early to judge the risk, but it's not too early to anticipate the problems. Congress needs to enable the program, but not to overspecify it. Somehow, the program has to anticipate the early adopters will be those people who are in a position to regard the loss of a hundred or two hundred dollars as no big deal (mostly richer ones) but to leave the door ajar for later entry of timid folks, poor folks, and those who will take no risk except on a sure thing. That means voluntary entry with graded incentives for late-comers (a dollar at birth, 2 dollars at age 10, 4 dollars at age 20, etc.) And it means avoidance of political control except to close it down if its managers misbehave, with the ability to re-open it after the loophole has been fixed. If it works, early adopters will have made a pile of money. And if it doesn't work, well, you only lost a few bucks.

What Are the Reasons to Believe Science Will Cure Some Significant Diseases in the Next Century? 1. In the first place, the National Institutes of Health research budget is currently $33 billion a year. It concentrates on basic research, leaving applied research to patent-seeking companies in the private sector. That is, drug companies and medical device makers. When the private sector produces a patent, the product price is initially high enough to pay for the research and some hefty profit; after a few years, the price comes down. If private sector research should ever seem to diminish, some sensible modification of the Kefauver "efficacy" requirement or its enforcement ought to kick-start it, again.

2. Let me tell you a personal story of a trip to an invitation-only investment seminar, limited to private foundations. On the opening day, the moderator said, "Let's get acquainted. Would everyone who represents less than $30 million dollars, please raise your hand." Of the roughly two hundred attendees, I was one of four who raised his hand. The Dean of the Harvard Business School was on my left, and the representative of the Bill Gates Foundation was on my right. I would estimate that ten times the amount of the Rockefeller Foundation was represented, and that four times the assets of that room would be found in the foundations of the rest of the country who were not attending the conference. By no means all of them are involved in medical research, but many of them fund universities and other research centers. The amount of money available for medical research in the next century is astounding, and it's America's collective bet on success.

3. A relative of mine took a PhD course in mathematics at MIT. He was the only American citizen among the 73 enrollees. The amount of medical research we can anticipate coming from abroad, is very considerable and may in time exceed our domestic production. There is no shortage of available resources, or talent, world-wide. Nor research opportunities, although few foreign countries have caught the American fever for "thinking big". We have gone from the discovery of the DNA helix to complete identification of the human genome, during my lifetime. Only 2% of disease has been connected to the genome, so attention is shifting to the "silent" protein of the cell. Disease can run, but it can't hide. There are lots of diseases, but fifty percent of medical

cost is associated with only ten diseases. So, find ,em and get rid of ,em, before we start to become impatient.

4. Nor do we foresee a labor shortage. Self-driving cars should be on the streets in a decade, following which people will summon fleets of them by cell phone, followed by a decline in accidents and accident insurance. Since his entire holding company is balanced on the float from auto insurance, it will be interesting to see how Warren Buffett addresses the issue. The leader of a very large investment company also predicts self-correcting computer code will soon cause wide-spread unemployment. This is all creative destruction. A third of the country will be retired without sufficient income to live on, but an ample pool of employees for terminal care of the others will surface.

But enough. A real early-adopter doesn' t need four reasons to adopt early, and a timid soul won't be persuaded by forty arguments. Only America has the bit in its teeth at the moment, and that seems to be part of our culture. Only America would gamble ridiculous amounts of money on research, assuming that timid gestures like Otto von Bismarck's health insurance plan would only worsen the problem, creating many more problems of its own. What sane person wants to rule the whole world, anyway?

SECTION FOUR:

GRAND SUMMARY

It's Time for a Grand Summary

This book will appear in print around the time of the November, 2016 presidential election, and therefore have little effect on its outcome. I expect the election to polarize both political parties still further on the Affordable Care Act, sucking all the oxygen out of the room, as the expression goes. It is likely to create a sort of lame duck situation during November and December, no matter who wins. Therefore, I decided to present a book which superficially seems to have little to say about the Affordable Care Act, in order to grasp the microphone first, about health issues which got ignored by the Affordable Care uproar. Even when discussion seems to focus on the A.C.A., trade-offs are blithely apt to ignore "germane-ness". And thus get to issues which have been debated very little, and pass very quickly. This book primarily attempts to do two things to re-focus attention:

1. To draw attention to the Health Savings Account legislation as a fall-back from almost any deadlock. HSA is already enacted, tested, and distributed. If Congress reaches a deadlock, the HSA is existing law, and anybody in a jam can simply go down the street and buy one. It's simple and cheap to get started, is approximately as inexpensive as any other health insurance, and you can discard it whenever you like. (Naturally I hope people will keep it.)

It does have a few flaws, which I hope Congress might correct. It unnecessarily limits buyers to people who are employed. That seems purposeless to me, while it prevents minor children from being enrolled, limits the deposit of funds to a fixed amount of their own money, and forces people out of the HSA at age 65. Forcing people to drop it as they acquire Medicare, impairs one of its most important virtues, the incentive to apply unspent money to retirement living, just at the time they are likely to retire. Some people will have other retirement sources and time-tables, and wish to defer use of some or all of them. Getting back to children, permitting deposits at birth would add at least twenty years to the compound interest period available preceding retirement, allowing the retirement fund to grow four times as large. Dropping the age and employment limits would not require more than a few sentences of amendment, and provide maximum flexibility.

2. We also portray universal Health Savings (and Retirement) funds as potentially "a string holding together a necklace of pearls". To do that requires major legislation, going far beyond emergency stop-gaps for deadlocks. It's potentially a program for health, phased in over a century, and including the possibility of even including ACA. Since one Congress cannot bind a successor, it provides a road map through ten or more changes of political control in Washington, adding or subtracting individual programs which sometimes have little relation with each other. As a matter of fact, if attachment is voluntary, you can have other parallel programs without attaching them, if you prefer.

By happenstance, reform could start with one "pearl" already in place. By the legislation's automatic transfer to an Individual Retirement Account at the onset of Medicare coverage, every subscriber in effect would immediately possess one of the essential ingredients of a lifetime health and retirement funding system. That even generates coherence, symbolizing prolonged longevity as a result of earlier health care. On the other hand, it implies the present configuration of Medicare is perpetual when it already has a number of features which should be changed. Therefore, it is essential to state at the outset that the string, the HRSA, intends to be kept as simple as possible, so that amendment complexity is concentrated into the "pearls" themselves. After doing so, the HSA can remain versatile enough to suffice for newborns, mentally handicapped and billionaires, alike. It might provide healthcare for prisoners in custody as well as the marooned Medicare copayment supplements. Some things wouldn't work and can be dropped without upsetting the whole system. The expression is KISS -- which they tell me means keep it simple, stupid.

The basic structure is to divide health finance into two parts, one for everyday routine expenditures, and the other for bare-bones, cheap, insurance -- for people who are too sick in bed to be bothered with haggling over finances. If there is anything left over at age 65, it can be spent for retirement, and serves as a life-long incentive to be frugal about health expenses. It's for everybody, not just some demographic group. If the government chooses to subsidize certain groups, then that becomes an independent topic, sharing a common framework, hanging separately from the necklace as it were. At the moment, its one serious technical flaw is to imply total control over investment policy lies in the hands of any corporation which manages it, leading eventually to suboptimal investment performance for customers. Also, limiting management to visible fees rather than invisible profit-competition should allow plenty of room for shopping between managers.

Having established the basic framework and pointed out its present main -- but correctable -- flaws (management control of investment, and mandatory management participation in profits), we added two potential pearls to the necklace. One is the two parts (80/20) of Medicare with its finances unified, and the other is to provide health coverage for children up to the age of 25. These are both sensitive topics, and may take protracted debate to get the mechanics right. When these two programs have finally got their books balanced by deciding who pays for what, they are ready for voluntary acceptance into HSAs, and they remain eligible to be tossed out if unexpected problems surface, once we get over any notion of infallibility. Balancing the books may include subsidies, but the subsidies for poor or the handicapped must reasonably result in balanced books. It is intended to be an insurance design, not a subsidy originator. A design, not a budget; the government may subsidize as it pleases without changing the design. The government has a right, even a duty, to provide for those who cannot provide for themselves. But deficit financing is not wise: if you are going to subsidize, subsidize the pearls, not the string. This wouldn't eliminate politics, it merely shifts politics to a less dangerous level.

At that point we now stop detailed planning, and merely list seven more "pearls" which might be added on the same terms. They would be special programs for difficult situations, like prisoners in custody, physically or mentally handicapped to the point of not being self-sufficient, and aliens within our borders. We are told the aggregate of these three groups alone is thirty million people.

When it comes time to negotiate the Affordable Care Act, between twenty and forty million more are eligible to become self-financed "pearls", after the ACA finds a way to balance its books. It is not intended to subsidize other subsidies linked to programs. That's the government's job. Unfortunately, the government has tended to raise prices for people struggling to pay their bills by subsidizing other people who cannot. The consequence is even more people cannot afford their own care, threatening to sink the lifeboat for everybody. If we are to subsidize the health care of some part of the population, let the money come from defense, or agriculture, or infrastructure, not from the quality of healthcare of some other person.

To continue the list, additional pearls for the future are the accumulated debts of fifty years of deficits, and the tax deduction-supported gifts of health insurance from employers to employees. I'd like to see some resolution of the mess left behind by *Maricopa Medical Society v. Arizona* decision of the Supreme Court. As these problems get worked out to be self-sufficient, they become eligible to become "pearls" as long as it remains clear this proposal in not a cross-subsidy vehicle. At the moment, the ACA shows no signs of adding anything to the HRSAs except more deficits, making solutions more difficult to find. Just because we see no end to problems, shouldn't keep us from getting started. In particular, when the ACA is addressed, out goes the oxygen from the room, diverting attention from anything except expedients. That should not be necessary. All of these problems can be worked on simultaneously.

* * *

It is now time to identify the financial maneuvers which promise partial success. It isn't true there is only one principle involved, but there is certainly one main one. Almost all of the magic of money creation in this proposal is provided by stretching out the time for income earning. A longer earning period takes advantage of the rock-solid principle of compound interest rising at the end of its investment period. To return to our oft-repeated formula, money earning 7% will double in 10 years, so 2,4, 8, 16 reaches 512x magnification in 90 years. From age 80 to 90 the money grows 128-fold., so an original investment of $100 grows from $25,600 to $51,200 between the ages of 80 and 90 or $2,560 per year for a $100 investment. That is, it's not growing at 7%; during those last 10 years it's growing at 256%. And it's not magic, it's just math. Furthermore, it's not new. The ancient Greek Aristotle complained about the unfairness of it because he was seeing it as a debtor. So that suggests a related strategy: wherever possible, position citizens as creditors, not as debtors.

What's new about this whole thing is the extension of longevity. In Aristotle's day, it was considered remarkable to live to be forty years old. In our era, life expectancy at birth is moving from 80 toward 90. So today it's not a pipe dream, it's a realistic strategy. But stretching it out automatically comes with problems, too. There's greater risk, fifty years of extra opportunity for someone to chisel it from you. History is replete with examples of kings who shaved gold coins, financiers who took more profit for themselves than for their investors, central banks who give you back a penny when you invested a dollar a century earlier. If you win a war, you might emerge better off; but if you lose a war you may be more like the seventy million people who died from wars in the past century, an experience which strongly favors having no wars, but otherwise doesn't seem to change things much. This risk/reward ratio strongly suggests we have neglected the necessary precautions required. So the proposals of earlier pages to balance the Medicare budget, etc., carry the risk that something or someone will come along and divert the money to other purposes. And without planning to forestall that, you have not got a workable plan.

That's the thinking underneath the dispersion of control to individual Health Savings Accounts, just as it is the reasoning behind resistance to consolidated systems of control, such as "single payer" systems as presently described by their proponents. They all just make it easier for your trusted agent to steal bigger amounts of money at one time. William Penn, the richest private landholder in recorded Western history, spent his days in debtor's prison because his steward falsely accused him of stealing the money from him. Robert Morris, the financial savior of our nation, likewise went to debtor's prison while the Governor of his state nearly sprained his hand signing over property deeds to himself. When the Federal Reserve was created in 1913, a dollar was a dollar;

now it is a penny. Nobody needs to explain what "pay to play" means. So, although we need much more ingenuity in devising safeguards for savers, we need to grit our teeth and allow some people to fail to take their opportunities. Countless teenagers who might have had a comfortable retirement will instead have the opportunity to smash up their red convertible on the way home from college. We absolutely must not deprive them of this risk, out of sympathy for its consequences. There will be plenty of Huns, Goths and Vandals watching what Rome does with its advantages.

* * *

Suffice it to say a billion dollars will turn anyone's head; Health Savings Accounts are already many times that size in aggregate. Although ownership is dispersed widely, it is only a matter of time before some stockholders organization is formed, ostensibly to protect the interests of HSA owners. There will be an eternal need to suggest tweaks in the law to adjust to new circumstances. There will be a need to monitor the performance of managers, and even to counter the power of regulators. Sneaky little laws will get thrown in the hopper, requiring alarms in the night. Someone who lost money will sue to recover it; someone will have to decide whether to settle or resist in court, ever mindful of precedents being set. Executives will demand extraordinary life-styles; someone will have to decide if their production warrants the rewards. Someone else will have to be fired for incompetence or venality, but he will find many friends to defend him. The methods of selection of the board of directors are vital issues, now and forever in the future. As much as anything, continuous publication of results ("sunlight") is vital to oversight. The directors of the oversight body should have a deep suspicion of the directors of the "pearls" and only limited pathways for promotion between the two. Every time, every single time a dereliction is discovered, the results should be published and morals drawn. Mr. Giuliani made a name for himself by policing broken windows, and it's still a very sound principle.

There is financial success, and then there is product quality, which is different. Organizations will undoubtedly be formed to monitor quality, and these will produce measureable monitoring results. An effort should be made to make a meaningful match between these two report cards, with comparable groups having access to each other's data. There should be observers from each discipline on the other's board, and possibly a few voting overlaps. Disparities between rankings in the two evaluations should be explored and evaluated, and at least one annual meeting should be composed of both kinds of boards, devoted to the interaction of cost and quality. This may prove particularly fruitful at moments when scientific advances cause major changes in underlying premises. On another level, dialog should be frequent between research groups like the NIH, to see if research parallels needs..

A particularly interesting comparison might result from contrasting the regions with their 20% copayment partner's performance. They should be very similar, but may not prove to be.

www.ingramcontent.com/pod-product-compliance
Lightning Source LLC
Chambersburg PA
CBHW031402180326
41458CB00043B/6585/J